Border Voices

on

BORDER RUINS

An Anthology from
Borders Writers' Forum

Edited by
Iona Carroll and Dorothy Bruce

River Tweed boulders

This anthology is a taster of the writing of members of Borders Writers' Forum on the theme of Border Ruins.

Edited by Iona Carroll and Dorothy Bruce

Further information on the Forum and its members can be found at www.borderwritersforum.com

Border Voices on Border Ruins: An Anthology from Border Writers' Forum Copyright ©Border Writers' Forum, November 2010.

British Library Cataloguing-in-Publication Data
A CIP catalogue record for this book is available from the British Library

ISBN 978-0-9567128-0-6

Published by
Border Writers' Forum
Greenbank
West End
Gordon
Berwickshire
TD3 6JP
www.borderwritersforum.com

The publishers acknowledge support from Scottish Borders Council

Printed and bound by Think Ink Ltd, 11-13 Phillip Road, Ipswich, Suffolk IP2 8BH

Border Voices on BORDER RUINS

Foreword by Stuart Kelly

I have just moved back to the Borders having spent eight years in Edinburgh. While in Edinburgh I wrote what I think of my Borders book (Scott-Land: The Man Who Invented A Nation). It seemed only right to return to the Borders while I work on my Edinburgh book, and returning left me with the profound sense that psychologically I had never left.

It is no surprise that Hugh MacDiarmid, the greatest 20th century writer from the Scottish Borders, once wrote: "there are plenty of ruined buildings in the world, but no ruined stones". The combination of historical dereliction – whether at the hands of Henry VIII's troops or modern capitalism – and geological permanence leaves an indelible impression on anyone who has lived in the area. The evidence of that lingering ambivalence, between past and present, between abandonment and recovery, between myth and history, is evident throughout this volume. Ruins are often spaces where the new can establish a foothold.

For any creative writer, perhaps the most valuable resource the Borders can offer is its borderline nature. It is, as Robert Leach says in his poem The Silence of the Sky, "motorways away". Although in the Minstrelsy of the Scottish Border, Sir Walter Scott wrote that "the accession of James to the English crown converted the extremity into the centre of his kingdom", this is a piece of wish-fulfilment. The Borders might not enjoy the "brand recognition" of the Highlands or the political influence of the Central Belt, but it maintains a unique standpoint; and often the view from the sidelines, the "dangerous edge of things", is a necessary perspective. The South African critic Breyten Breytenbach has written in praise of "The Middle World" – the place which is not the Centre but "by definition and vocation peripheral; it is other, living in the margins, the live edges". Breytenbach characterises the "uncitizen" of the Middle World as superstitious, proud, hybrid, chameleon, disloyal, as interested in form as in concept, an "inventive and transformative reporter of fact" and always "obliged to create concepts: the security of the known is forbidden to him, and this is why fundamentalists of all stripes will abhor and wish to expectorate the very name". It seems to me as if the Borders has all the essential qualities to belong to the Middle World. Walter Scott, again, captures something of this when he wrote about the shock the publication of the Minstrelsy caused: "when the book came out, the imprint, Kelso, was read with wonder by amateurs of typography, who had never heard of such a place, and were astonished at the example of handsome printing which so obscure a town had produced". Sometimes being away from the big lights allows subtler flames to flourish.

   As we enter the era of Coalition Austerity, groups such as the Borders Writers Forum will have a crucial role to play in sustaining and promoting all the arts. Indeed, I set up the Forum at a time when the Council discontinued the funding of a Writer in Residence, and I am glad that it continues to provide a space for diverse voices to be heard.

Stuart R. Kelly

Border Voices on BORDER RUINS

Contents

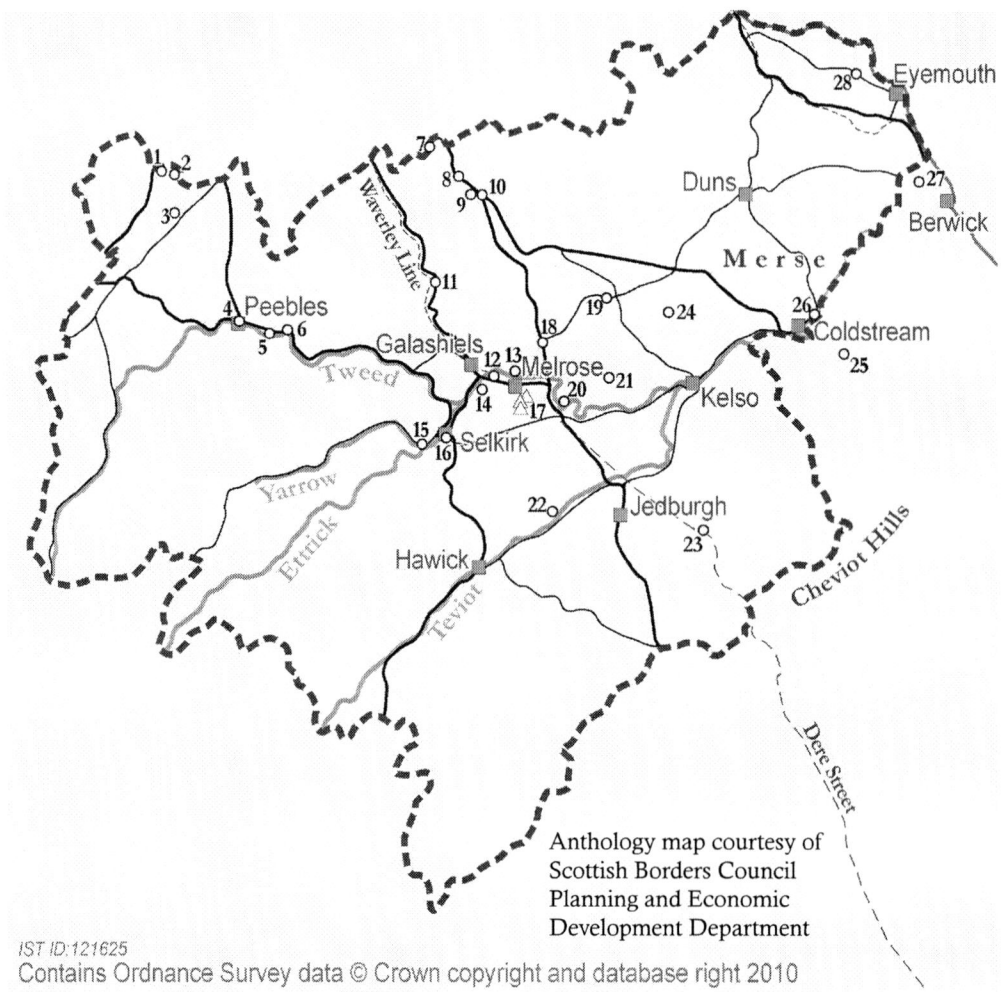

Anthology map courtesy of
Scottish Borders Council
Planning and Economic
Development Department

1. Kitleyknowe	15. Philliphaugh
2. Harlawmuir	16. Kirk o' the Forest
3. Macbiehill	17. Eildon Hills
4. Cross Kirk	18. Rhymers Tower
5. Horsburgh Castle	19. Greenknowe Tower
6. Nether Horsburgh Tower	20. Dryburgh Abbey
7. Soutra Aisle	21. Smailholm Tower
8. Channelkirk	22. Fatlips Castle & Minto Crags
9. Oxton	23. Whitton Edge
10. Carfraemill	24. Hume Castle
11. Stow	25. Flodden Field
12. Tweedbank	26. Lennel Kirk
13. Gattonside	27. Halidon Hill
14. Abbotsford	28. Coldingham

Melrose, Kelso and Jedburgh Abbeys are in appropriate towns.

The reddle man

by Bridget Khursheed

the first white blooms on a bank
the diagonal cut of the hedgecutter
each sliced to leave a cup
of fibres not flowers

a red man scans the branch line
nobody's garden
gathering nettles for a poultice
to ease his dye's sting

his profession written in his face
and his hands
all that is visible
signs of the sheep trade

his alchemy to mark
fertility in the ram's harness
his science to improve
the duration of the stain

that holds him back
girls flirt but call him de'il
behind his back none
want to know his business

unread, he has passed by
and so has the train
but before any lambing
the blackthorn still shine white

Note: Reddle or raddle is the name of the dye used to mark ownership of sheep
and, when contained in a harness (or raddle), to show which ewes in a flock have
been covered by the ram. The dyers who used to make it by hand and the railway
have both long since left the Borders.

Paradise Here: A Vision in Ruins

By Carol Norris

Dark and woolly you became,
Goddess, statue, glowing stone,
My star, still and effulgent,
Cased in ice shine ready to burst.

My ice stone radiant herald
Of the North Pole Star, you are now a shadow,
Small in a corner, mildewed, grey,
Dour, sour, no hour came for you, for me, the world.

No glorious new sun shone overhead in winter,
Nor rose victorious from the West,
While poised on her axis the world stood still,
Till a new heaven and a new earth came.

My ice stone who once glittered
With the raiment of the North Pole Star,
Now I see you as you are
No harbinger of light but dark.

My Bright Herald, you are a delusion,
But almost lost myself in losing you,
No glowing stone or burning bush:
This a stone; that a bush.

Ageless Stone
by Pamela Gordon Hoad

'If these stones could speak', you hear them say as they maunder around on their pilgrimages, gawping at us wherever we happen to be, now at the beginning of their twenty-first century. Whimsical nonsense! Well, of course, we could tell them a tale or two, going back over aeons and aeons since we were cast up from the furnace at the heart of the earth, melded by shrinking sheets of ice, lapped by the rivers which have smoothed our jagged edges and fashioned some of us into elegant, multi-coloured pebbles fit to hang on a necklace.

What they actually mean, these chattering visitors who pay homage to some mysterious god called Tourism, is that we have witnessed what their own ancestors got up to in the few thousand years humans have tramped about among us. Anthropocentric they are; always have been, thinking we were put here to serve their purposes, ever since they first knapped us into arrow heads and tools for skinning the deer they killed. Later they started to quarry us out of the ground and pile us up to provide shelters for themselves and byres for the animals they learned to nurture for their hides and milk and best rump steak.

Some of us, round here, were shaped and dressed nearly two thousand years ago when the short-skirted Romans came (forerunners of those kilt-wearers, I reckon). They put up sophisticated buildings with columns and squared lintels and they incised a few of my mates with names and dates in honour of their imperial deities, albeit they were mostly dubious characters as I've heard. Another novel idea they had – milestones, stood on end by the side of their bolt-straight streets, organising the countryside into measured parcels between their towns. Others of us became scraped and rutted by their chariot wheels racing over the paved roadways and pounded by the thump of legionaries' creaking boots.

My own story, from the point of view of human history, started a bit later, after the Romans, in the time of mystery and myth that they're still finding out about, whenever they dig up a pagan torque or a simple Celtic cross. I was jutting out of the hillside, where I'd been quite comfortable since the last eruption of what became the triple-headed – but extinct – volcano. My peaceful existence was shattered when tonsured clerics came to the valley, from further south in the Kingdom of Northumbria (which claimed the area then), and they started to build an abbey out of wattle and daub and timber. They sited it on the bare headland, thrust into the meandering river, kissed by the rising sun as it lifts above the humped hill to the east which was my resting place. They wanted their church to be grander than the hovels they lived in, with a thatched cruck roof and set on a foundation course of stone, so a crowd of us were hauled down the slope and across the water to begin our working lives in the construction industry.

The man Cuthbert, whom they later called a saint, was Prior at Mailros, as they called the abbey, and years later they brought his relics for safekeeping when the Norsemen invaded. During the monastery's heyday the monks came into the church every few hours and I'd hear them chanting and praying in some barbaric tongue, not unlike the way the Romans had spoken but less refined. One cleric who was especially revered saw visions of Heaven and Hell and carried on about them interminably. He sought redemption by plunging into the river at mid-winter, among the ice floes. They said that demonstrated his sanctity. Bit of an idiot, I thought him. Still, I liked the idea of their religion being founded on a rock: good sense that is.

I stayed in my position at the church, third block from the south door, second row above ground, for a few hundred years, even when the walls on top of us were burnt down and rebuilt. I still have a singe mark at one end from that fire. I continued there while the whole place fell apart. The unoccupied monastic cells, leaning against the boundary bank, collapsed and soon bushes were growing up among the debris. Pigeons flew into the church through the narrow window slits and holes in the roof and they splattered the neat cobbled floor with their unholy detritus. It became smelly and shabby and I was ashamed to be associated with such squalor. I was glad when a local fellow carried me off to be part of the doorstep in his ramshackle hut, down by the clack mill, and there I stayed until his great grandson's time.

He was a bright lad, that Ernald, I will say that, and he had an eye to the main chance. As a boy he showed a rare talent for whittling sticks and cutting grotesque faces on logs and then he started scratching away at some of the softer stones in the river bank. He heard that the king at that time, the King of Scots by then, was intent on founding a new abbey not far away. It wasn't to be the simple sort of place old Mailros had been but a vast establishment, with a soaring church of finely dressed ashlar and high traceried windows. Stone masons would be needed to chisel and chip for years ahead and my young owner determined he'd be part of it.

First he needed to decamp nearer the building site, to the new steading, as they called it, where the workmen had their base. He wasn't the sort to waste what he already had, so he dismantled the old cottage and trundled me and my mates in a one-wheeled barrow the mile or so to this hamlet where he reassembled us. I got to be part of the lintel above the small window then but, to make me fit, he squared off my corners and carved a rather ragged cross on my underside. I gathered he was practising his mark, his mason's mark, which he would put on his fine carving when they allowed him to do skilled work at the abbey.

It was only centuries later that I saw that wonderful edifice during the time of its glory. Ernald's cottage was squat and low-doored, screened by trees from the site of the new abbey, but I heard of the corbels and capitals, buttresses and bosses, all demonstrating craftsmanship and artistry, and for many years I begrudged those chunks of masonry their good fortune. I envied them their celebrity, part of a renowned and sacred place, on public view as superb examples of sculpted stone, cunningly faceted, delicately carved. Royalty visited, kings were buried there – or just bits of them some-times – and lavish ceremonies were held in the precincts. Yet it all proved transitory, as all human matters do.

The glimpse I had of the majestic rose-pink abbey came when it was my turn to be reused. Ernald was long dead and many other workmen had lived in his home but it became dilapidated and was judged too small for modern tastes. They came with mallets and mattocks to demolish it and it was then I sustained the injury which left me with a broken side. Only the symmetrical blocks were taken to repair the great cloister and the rest of us were carted down to the ford across the river, lugged over the meadows on the other side and part-way up the gorse covered slopes which looked towards the distant abbey. Further along the ridge the tenants of the monks tended the orchards which grew the finest cherries in Scotland, so they said. The Prior thought himself a connoisseur of such fruit and made frequent visits to sample its quality. He decreed that a grange should be built to store the produce grown on that sunny incline so I found myself thrust, amongst a perfect hotchpotch of inferior masonry, to be part of a common barn. I admit I was distressed to discover my destiny and to be compelled to face across the valley, looking towards those arrogant, hallowed stones of King David's splendid abbey.

Before long, however, I came to recognise the advantages of my humble, utilitarian existence. The abbey had been attacked before but the great desecration occurred when an army from the south fired the town and smashed the monastery buildings. My relatives who had held positions of distinction in the walls of bakehouse, malthouse, dormitory and refectory were battered and broken. The church was pillaged and local people carried off fancy niches and decorated vaulting to ornament their homes, just as had happened when old Mailros was destroyed. Years later other fanatics went round knocking the heads off statues, believing all that inanimate beauty was somehow sinful. Mind you, I chuckled to think of some of those pompous carvings without their stuck-up faces.

Ah well! I watched it all from afar and then my own time of greatest ignominy came. The grange was abandoned and we lapidaries subsided, one by one, to be lost among nettles and ferns. I rested in the middle of a thistle bed for many years, only vaguely aware of the growing noise around us. Humans brought machines onto the earth and booming monsters into the sky and I found it all very bewildering. Then came the day the field was cleared and all stones were bundled together and left in a great heap in one corner. New buildings went up and some of us were lifted, cleaned up a bit and used by the dykers to make a 'feature' wall – dry stone, they call it, albeit we're wet stones, as usual, when it rains.

So here I am, still working, at the top of this fancy edging to a little garden. As my rather crude neighbour puts it, they stuck me 'arse uppards', so that cross young Ernald chipped out so long ago is plain for everyone to see. People have talked about it. 'Might be a mason's mark,' one of the brighter ones said. 'I'm not sure,' some expert replied. 'It's only rough. Might have been done by a plough,' Much they know. I'd like to tell them. If only stones could speak.

The stone that inspired the story.

The Silence of the Sky
By Robert Leach

Grass blades – soft razors
Stroking my jugular;
Sod lumps – chunky
On shoulders, backbone.
In this circle of stones,
Grey slabs, gnarly,
Tottering, lean
To self-destruction.
I hear only
Waterfalls of blackbird song,
And sheep bleating feebly
Fields off. The low blue
Washes my eyelids. Silence
In the sky. And you
Get on with your business
Motorways away.

The Border Abbeys
by Eileen Thornton

Four of the most beautiful abbeys in the Scottish Borders were built within close proximity of each other. Built to the Glory of God during the twelfth century, all but one was founded by the pious King David Iof Scotland.

Kelso Abbey, founded in 1128, is the oldest of the four and was built while David was still an Earl. Originally he wanted the abbey to be built in the nearby Border Town of Selkirk, so in 1113 he brought thirteen monks from Tiron in Northern France to do the task. However in 1124, after he was proclaimed King, he changed his mind and produced a new charter stating that his abbey should be near to the Royal Burgh of Roxburgh.

Kelso Abbey stands on the banks of the River Tweed, now renowned for its Salmon fishing. Despite its ruinous state, the majestic building still shows signs of beautiful Romanesque architecture. In fact King David was so proud of his abbey that after the death of his son in 1153, he ignored the usual burial site at Dunfermline for Scottish kings and heirs, and declared that his beloved son would be buried at Kelso.

Furthermore, this one time magnificent abbey was the most important in the area. In 1160, John, 5th Abbot of Kelso Abbey, was bestowed the Mitre by the Pope, giving him precedence over all other abbots. Also, in 1460 the infant James III was crowned here following the untimely death of his father, James II, who was killed when one of his own cannons exploded during a battle at Roxburgh. Moreover the Coronation of James IV was also held in this abbey.

However, because of its close proximity to the border, Kelso Abbey, which at one time was the largest of all four Borders abbeys, was constantly under attack by the English. Nevertheless, somehow the abbey managed to survive 400 years of violence and it was only finally destroyed in 1545 during the Reformation. On the orders of King Henry VIII, the Earl of Hertford reduced the abbey to rubble.

Today many people still believe the abbey to be the most important building in Kelso. It was only the sudden influx of people seeking work on the building that caused the rise of a whole new town.

Therefore, without the abbey, the Kelso area may have remained a mere suburb of Roxburgh. As a result there is now no trace of the original town of Roxburgh. Now, point-to-point horse racing is held every year on the very spot where the ancient town once stood.

In 1136, King David arranged for a group of Cistercian Monks from Rievaulx in Yorkshire to begin work on another abbey. His original plan was for the abbey to be built at Old Melrose, a few miles west of Kelso. However, a new site was sought when the land was found to be unsuitable.

Melrose Abbey was dedicated to the Blessed Virgin in 1146 and soon afterwards became one of the wealthiest in all Scotland. In the fourteenth century, Robert the Bruce was so impressed with the abbey that after a devastating attack, he ordered a large sum of money to be made available so that it could be rebuilt. Furthermore, his dying wish was that his heart should be buried there.

In 1921, a lead casket containing an embalmed heart was unearthed. However, as there was no proof that the heart was that of Robert the Bruce, it was reburied. But in 1996 the heart was removed again for further tests and this time, using more updated science, it was established that it was indeed the heart of The Bruce. Consequently it was reburied in the Chapter House in ceremonious style.

Today Melrose Abbey is in ruins. Nevertheless, it is still well worth a visit as much of the intricate detail of the stonemasons has survived down the centuries. Furthermore for those romantics among us, Sir Walter Scott, who lived close by at Abbotsford House, once said that 'Melrose Abbey is best seen by moonlight'.

On the other hand, the Abbey at Jedburgh, situated in the heart of the town, was originally founded as a priory in 1138. However, only a few years later, it was raised to the status of abbey.

In 1285, the wedding of King Alexander III to Yoland de Dreux was held in the abbey. A legend tells of a ghostly apparition that appeared during the wedding feast and mingled with the guests. However, several of the guests were very superstitious, and believed it to be a bad omen for the happy couple. Their fears were proved right when the King was found dead at the foot of the cliffs at Kinghorn in Fife only a few months later.

The main body of this splendid abbey remains almost intact, despite the numerous attacks during the wars of independence.

Jedburgh Abbey

High above the beautiful west door, an impressive rose window can still be seen. Even after the abbey's final destruction in 1545 on the orders Henry VIII, it continued to be used as a church until the Marquis of Lothian donated a new church to the town in the late nineteenth century. It is firmly believed that Jedburgh Abbey is one of the finest examples of early Gothic in all Scotland.

Of all the four abbeys, Dryburgh must be the most beautifully situated. Surrounded by trees, the abbey is quietly tucked away from the hustle and bustle of the nearby towns of Kelso, Jedburgh and Melrose and even today there is still a monastic feel about the place.

The abbey was founded by Sir Hugo de Moreville Lord of Lauderdale and Constable of Scotland in 1150, and is believed to be on a site of earlier religious connections. Nevertheless, despite its remoteness, the abbey still received its fair share of attacks during its history. Edward II caused severe damage in 1322 and there was further devastation by Richard II in 1385. However despite the devastating attack in 1544, by the Earl of Hertford, much of the abbey still remains intact, especially in the east cloisters.

In 1832, Sir Walter Scott was buried in the chapel and lies beside his wife Charlotte, who was buried some six years earlier. Other members of his family lie close by. Similarly Field Marshal Earl Haig, Commander of the British Forces during the First World War, is buried a short distance from the Scott Family. It is only the descendants of these families together with the Erskines, one-time owners of the abbey, who have the right to be buried at Dryburgh Abbey.

Finally all four of the abbeys, which have survived 900 years of turmoil, are now regarded as Scotland's Heritage and are maintained by Historic Scotland.

Greenknowe Tower

By Vee Freir

Beyond a sea of nettles
And scented meadow-sweet
The tended tinder path
Gives passage to Greenknowe Tower,
A roofless ruin in manicured lawn surround.
Angle-corner turrets with sandstone,
Red to break grey Border uniform,
As the heavy iron gate
Creaks open with gloomy sound
Reveals the dark below.
The vaulted kitchen there
Its grated windows slitted
Barely showing the dank floor,
While spiraling upwards the stone stair
Leads to once where Seton sat,
Now open to the elements
Where pigeons make home
Among the weed filled lintels;
Windows wide to the country
On all sides, and distant trees
As shield to prying village eyes

Greenknowe Tower

All Because of a Girl Called Hayley
by Oliver Eade

Fiction

She didn't even turn round for a last look. Just stepped up onto the carriage and slammed the door shut. The train containing his wife curled out of Berwick station, and once gone, it seemed like he might as well stay forever on that platform staring at the timeless ruin of the city wall, thinking about his personal ruin: his life. She'd been his life, and he'd always assumed their love to be something permanent. Now it was little more than a scar cutting his existence in two. Permanent, but a dead permanence ... like that old wall.

God, what the hell had he done to make everything go so horribly wrong?

He'd brought her to the Borders *because* of its ruins and history. History had been her thing before Hayley came on the scene. She had a brilliant academic career ahead of her. So *why*? Had the childlessness of their seven-year old marriage encouraged Hayley? Doubtless *she* blamed everything on him and his work, though never said as much. In fact, of late she never said much to him at all. For which *he* blamed Hayley. He'd often thought about ways of killing the girl after realising the effect she had on his wife. *Now* he thought of only one thing. To dispose of her in the cruellest way possible: death by burning and the council tip.

Everything had been carefully planned. After the drive up from Suffolk they'd spend a night in Jedburgh, see the abbey, move on to Kelso, another abbey, Smailholm Tower, Dryburgh, Melrose; then take in the defunct mills of Selkirk and Galashiels and the ruined church and old bridge at Stow. Using history, they would revisit their past, put things back on the right track and rebuild the crumbling ruin of their marriage. She might even be persuaded to use her writing skills to become a historical novelist. Forget Hayley, perhaps?

Forget Hayley? If only! Those piercing eyes that never left him, that pert up-turned nose, sweet little chin and ruby lips. Could he ever destroy her?

Things never work out according to plan. The more ruins they visited the more distant she became, as though reminding him, and in a small bookshop in Melrose they saw Hayley. That did it! On the final leg of their Borders tour he decided to pull out his last stop. He'd seen the ruined Peel tower on a promontory near the River Tweed as they headed for Peebles. On the way back, with not one word having been spoken all morning, he drove the car up onto a verge near the ruin.

Not much of a building, but could it provide a turning point?

'Let's sit there a while,' he said, looking across the road at the old tower. 'Enjoy those rolls I got in Peebles. Years since we last had a picnic together.'

'That ancient pile of stones? Come off it!'

'Looks sort of romantic to me. Think of its past. Christ knows what might have happened within those old walls. *Real* history! Who knows, you could get inspiration for a historical novel? The life of a reiver must've been quite something ... intrigue, deceit, wall-to-wall fighting ... thieving ... and their women, you know ... they ...'

'They what?'

He thought about those Borders women of the past, so dutifully subservient to their men-folk. Would it have been different for the two of them back then, within the walls of the Peel tower? Might its past rub off onto them even now, if they were to sit together, their backs to that wall? Not that he wanted her to be subservient. Just ... well, a *little* responsive. That's all he asked.

'Dunno! Anyway, I'm hungry. And you could ... you know ...'

'What?'

'Write a historical novel. Starting here in the Borders. Inside that Peel tower. As it used to be.'

'Bloody couldn't! Hayley would have kittens!'

'For God's sake, can't you forget flipping Hayley? For an hour or two?'

He *would* plan Hayley's death if she refused to speak to him. Work it out to the last detail, including the burning and disposal of the ashes.

Soon they were sitting with their backs to the tower wall staring in silence at the river. His hunger had left him and both rolls lay untouched on his bent-up knees.

'I've been thinking, Sara,' he said at last. 'We need to do something together for a change. Whilst you were involved with Hayley in that bookshop in Melrose ... I ...'

He flicked away an ant that was wandering uncomfortably close to his foot. How he wished he could have done the same to Hayley.

'Well, if you were to write a novel about reivers and stuff, I could help with the research. Things should be less busy for me at the hospital now I've a new colleague. Look, I know I've been rather ...'

'It's over, John!' she interrupted, cutting into his sentence.

'No ... Sara ... please, hear me out...'

'I'm expecting a baby. *His!*'

He looked at Sara, at the river, the sky ... his feet ... the ant ... searching for something that might tell him this was only a bad dream. Reality stared back at him wherever he looked.

'*His?*'

'I ... I was going to tell you sooner, John, honest, but ...'

'Wait a minute, Sara. I'm lost here. *His* baby? What ... I mean, who on earth ...?'

'Pat.'

She'd turned to face him. She was crying, but averted her gaze when their eyes met.

'Your agent? But she's a bloody woman!'

'Pat? He's a man all right! Very much a man. You never asked, never seemed the slightest bit interested in what I did. Oh God, John, I wanted to tell you at the time ... three months ago, before I toured the States with Hayley, but ...'

'Damn Hayley! How could I know Pat was a man? *Jesus Christ!*'

'You never asked and I felt so confused ... lonely ... but when I found out I was expecting last week ... I ...'

'You love him?'

Sara paused before shrugging her shoulders.

'But how can you be so sure it's ...?'

'We were together for two months during my tour. He was the only one who made love to me. Besides ...'

'Yeah, yeah! No need to bloody rub it in! *Jesus!* A baby by another man? Sara, I ...'

'Look ... I think I should just take the train back. Sort out stuff at home ...'

'*Whose* bloody home?'

'Get my things together and ...'

'Move in with the bastard? Oh God, Sara!'

He too was crying.

' Don't know! Like I said, I've been confused. Go to Mum's, perhaps.

Look ... I really ...'

'I'll kill him!'

'That wouldn't change things! John, I'm so sorry. It happened, and that's all I can say!'

'*Happened?* Christ, only because you bloody let it! And all because of a girl called Hayley, the little bitch.'

Not a word was exchanged until they reached Berwick station where she repeated 'I'm so sorry,' over and over without turning to look at him.

Nothing made sense. The ruins, Hayley ... and now a baby by a man he'd always assumed to be a woman! His mind in a whirl, he drove back across the Borders towards the little town of Melrose. He'd buy every Hayley book they had in that bookshop, take them to the ruined Peel tower and watch her suffer and burn with all the hatred he could muster. He'd go to every bookshop in the Borders, buy up stocks of Hayley books, burn them, then set off around the country to rid the rest of the world of Hayley. Not even on Amazon would the ruddy girl be able to flaunt her silly grinning face that had bought Sara world fame and ruined his life.

At Home with Hayley; Hayley on Holiday; Hayley at the Zoo; Hayley the Girl Detective ....

Hayley just went on and on and on, the little cow!

Christ, he'd make Hayley suffer for what she'd done to them! Was burning alone good enough? Should he soak every book in cat's piss and vinegar before burning it?

Wet things don't burn and their cat was as dead as their marriage!

Hayley, Hayley, Hayley!

He could think of nothing else as he sped towards Melrose, his foot pressed full down on the accelerator. Hayley and the life she'd destroyed formed a dark cloud filling every corner of his mind. Hayley's big smiley eyes taunted him through the windscreen, blocking out the road, the fields of corn, rape, cows ... and the trees.

On seeing the police car waiting outside their home, Sara's first thought was for Pat. *He'd* carried out his threat and killed her lover! The truth seemed a thousand times more terrible, not softened by the words 'he'd not have felt a thing when the car hit the tree'. And it got worse. Returning to the Borders to identify the body was like 'unbearable' taken far beyond the limits of endurance, but she

Horsburgh Tower, near Glentress

stayed on there, in the Borders, close to the ruins and to him. She'd finished with Pat. That's what she was trying to say when she told him about the baby, but somehow only her anger showed and it was turned against him for not destroying Hayley sooner ... not preventing all that ruination.

She had the child in the Borders. She bought a house there and she read about the reivers, their lives and the ruins they'd left behind. She wrote that novel. It became a best-seller.

Her daughter's name is Hayley.

Fatlips Castle

By Bridget Khurseed

The plan to import cedar benches
from which game could be targetted
thwarted by the rutted approach
to modernization until

ten men paid in seed potatoes advance
to carry the lumber, lady's cushions
embroidered in medieval scenes,
a bird cage, trunks containing Coalport

and silver, 3 lanterns, blankets, sundries
and a stuffed bear.
The latter slightly damaged in the mouth
on the ascent; a tooth squint.

But the castle tower itself shrugs off
all the prettifying; no good applying lipstick
to this mouth and topping the keep
with machicolation,

dripstones on the arrow slits –
what went on here slips through the stones
hot trod of ponies in the night
a landsmann cuirass lost at Bosworth

crammed over a Turnbull's head
punch drunk his smile swollen with blows
and head from stolen grain
smell of the latrine and the speckle of blood lost.

Victorian stencilling is washed away
stumped maquillage in border rain
bricked up door broken by boys and girls
reiving for a contemporary lay.

Note: Fatlips Castle is a 16th century peel tower in Roxburghshire situated at the top of Minto Crags, above the River Teviot. It was built by the Turnbulls of Barnhills, notorious Border reivers. In 1545, it was burnt by Earl of Hertford during the War of the Rough Wooing. It was restored in 1857 as a shooting lodge and private museum, while the interior was renovated by Sir Robert Lorimer in 1897–8. The building was in use until the 1960s. It is now, however, once again in ruins.

Kirk O' The Forest
by Tom Murray

When does the place that you live, but weren't born, become home?
Is it measured in years? Or does the place of your birth and more
than likely the formative years of your childhood always hold sway?
In other words can you ever really put down roots anywhere else?
Answers on a postcard please!

All this is a bit of a clue to the fact that where I live now, Selkirk in
the Scottish Borders, isn't the place of my birth.

I was born and brought up in the Central Belt but have lived in
the Borders for almost half my life now.

So what would I write if I sent a postcard to myself?

Dear Tom.
Digging deep and putting down fresh roots.
You're here.
Tom.

Digging deep. That is the key for me.

Digging deep and finding the connection with roots already
there.

Fresh roots have to be nourished and encouraged and for me let-
ting the history of the town enter my soul and feel it connect with
the living present started the process.

Selkirk town is like a calm river on a windless summer's day at
times. Other times it is a buzz of lorries and cars winding their way
through the too narrow streets and twisting their way around tight
corners. This snake like progress is because the A7 cuts through
the centre of Selkirk leading the one way to Carlisle, the other way,
Edinburgh. Other times it is a buzz of tourists searching, maybe, for
momentary peace from the rush of city life.

If that is what they're looking for they should head up Kirk Wynd,
just off Market Place, to the Kirk O The Forest and the old graveyard.
That would be the picture on the front of the postcard.

Here the remains of the old church dominate the graveyard
and give testament to the history of Selkirk folk through the ages.

Graves and memorials here remembering folk from the thirteenth to the twentieth century. Graves and memorials all different shapes and sizes, some grand and imposing, most not. It is a graveyard which has houses along one edge, a car park along another and a road outside its main gate. Still it seems detached from all of these things.

An oasis of stillness. Noises that are barely yards away hardly intrude. Or maybe that's my imagination too busy making connections between the people lying here and the living souls going about their daily life yards away...and myself.

The graveyard occupies different levels not only regarding the ground level but in the people buried.

Death it is said is the great leveller.

Maybe.

Morbid though it may seem I think it's in the graveyards that you get a real sense of how a town came to be the place you live in now. Much more so than in history books.

The Borders is rightly famous for its four abbeys at Melrose, Dryburgh, Kelso and Jedburgh but the ruins of this old church I think hold as much interest as any of them.

On the famous folk side of things it was here they say that William Wallace was made Guardian of Scotland in 1298. It's also here that some of the maternal ancestors of Franklin D Roosevelt, President of United States of America during the Second World War, are buried. On his mother's side he was related to the Murrays of Philiphaugh. The Murrays have a whole alcove to themselves in the church. A mini Westminster Abbey with vines curling up the crumbling walls for added effect. Here the Lords and Ladies and Generals, the good and the bad are buried.

One of the (maybe) bad of the clan was the 'Outlaw Murray.' John Murray (could he be a relation??!!) killed in 1510.

Other famous folk include Andrew Park the brother to the Explorer Mungo Park.

This is only one level though.

For when you step though the archway gate leading into the graveyard you step out of the twenty first century and travel back through time and get a sense that it's not just the great and the good that make up history and are responsible for the progress and changes that take place through the centuries.

And changes there have been. The Borders, including Selkirk, are a bit like the surrounding hills. You think they're not moving or changing. But like the earth, or life under those still waters, things are changing and developing all the time.

Like yourself settling into the rhythm of the place you don't notice because you're moving as well, changing, developing.

Putting down roots.

In this graveyard you get an idea of all the people who have gone before. Not only the rich and famous but the many that walked the same streets as them.

And you.

All living and dying and passing on their hopes and dreams down the centuries.

That's where I make the connection. The past is not a foreign land. Social conditions, even language might have been different but those hopes and dreams and the feeling of struggling to get by are fundamentally the same.

For to get a true sense of this place you must not only take on board all that life that has gone before but remember that life that is taking place only a few hundred yards away with the cars and lorries twisting and turning along the main A7. Connect up the past with the people a few yards away coming and going along Market Place, disappearing down alleyways, and shortcuts, that have been there and known for centuries. Streets, alleyways and shortcuts that have been trod by feet some of whose memory lies in the Kirk O'The Forest cemetery. Maybe some of those feet were walking hand in hand with loved ones. Maybe some were running for their lives or from the law, not wanting to come before Sir Walter Scott in the local courtroom.

Whatever soon all those now hurrying, or stopping to chat on the twenty first century Market Place, will join the ghost walk and be replaced by future generations following in their footsteps. For although ghosts and cemeteries are associated with night and dread I think the ghosts come out during the day, as they did in life, not at night. They walk the same streets they always walked. They walk beside us shaking their heads at our so familiar tales of worry and woe. They are like spirits caught in the background of photographs.

I stand before a grave now and wonder about the person lying there. Most of the markings have been scraped away by time. Like a lot of these old gravestones.

Still you can make the connection with the people who lived the history. All you have to do is take a rest for a moment from the daily rush and acknowledge that they existed. That they're not really truly dead and gone as long as the gates of this graveyard are kept open for folk to discover and step back in time for a short period.

So to answer my own question I believe you can put down roots in a place where you weren't born. Make the connection between past and present, the past contained in the present. Wherever you are.

Kirk O' The Forest

Fusion
by Dorothy Bruce

His hands were used first, spreading three blobs of shiny paint
squeezed onto the canvas. Mixing, pushing out towards the edges,
deftly stroking into position. This was nothing like a child painting,
as some of those watching claimed. It was deliberate, controlled.
The image was already in his head. Before starting, he psyched
himself up for the work, letting shapes, colours, atmosphere soak
into his mind and his hands. Acute observation. Not just eyes, but
all his senses alert, sampling the scene, discarding all but the
essential, retaining the essence. The image to be captured wasn't
two dimensional, wasn't static. So he understood how things
worked, moved. How each element functioned. How each aspect
interacted with the whole. It was the fusion of him as a person, his
skill and knowledge, with that whole which coaxed his painting
into existence.

A small curious crowd gathered nearby.

'What's he doing?' a woman asked.

'Painting a picture of the abbey,' another woman replied.

'He's not much of a painter, is he?'

'He's quite well known,' a man behind responded. 'Victor Tennant.
Haven't you heard of him?'

The woman shook her head. 'No painter I know puts on paint like
that, with their hands. It's just a mess.'

Someone laughed.

The man realised his comment wouldn't make any difference
to the woman but her told her anyway, 'He's known as Vert. His
name's Victor Edward Rutherford Tennant, so he signs his paintings
Vert.'

The woman looked at him, unimpressed. 'Bloody silly name to
saddle yourself with, if you ask me.'

Victor always considered the abbreviation rather good, thinking
the French word for green highly appropriate for an artist who
worked mainly in landscapes. As a child, his parents took him on
Sundays to Glasgow's Kelvingrove Museum to see stuffed animals
and skeletons, steam engines and bits of boats. They bored him
to tears. Literally. One time he wandered off, unnoticed by his

parents, and found the paintings. With a look of concentration, he stood looking up, fascinated. Cubism, surrealism, any work that saw life in a different way, appealed to him. He hadn't sought any explanation of why these paintings depicted the world differently. To him they were nerve-tinglingly exciting, reminding him of challenging games or puzzles. That was enough without external explanation. A loner, a misfit even then, obviously. With half the museum staff searching for him, his parents were furious when he was eventually run to ground. They couldn't understand what he was doing, looking at paintings instead of other exhibits. As far as Victor was concerned, they retained this lack of understanding of him and his work for the rest of their lives.

Given the early impact, it was surprising his own work hadn't veered in the direction of cubism or surrealism. Instead the Impressionists, van Gogh, even the Scottish Colourists had influenced his style. And though he painted the occasional work with figures, it was landscape that captivated him. He loved the undulating Borders countryside, the rust, red earth a constant reminder of its rich history, and frontline status, for centuries a bloody battleground.

Like a trained athlete he limbered up, freeing his mind of all but the work before him. Focussing. There was a routine. Easel erected, canvas secured, paints sorted, the colours he would use to bring the scene alive already known.

Then an explosion of concentrated energy set a fusion of mind and hands into the fray. By turns aggressively pummelling then caressing the canvas, cajoling from its fusion with the paint the effect centred in his mind. More colour was added, integrated by hand or long handled brush. Moving in towards the canvas for hand work, stepping back to wield the brush and see the bigger picture.

The mellow stones of the abbey around him belied its ravaged history. Through the centuries the fusion of assets and attributes gave the place its depth of character, its soul. St Aidan's and St Cuthbert's association attracted the white monks to the site beside the mighty River Tweed, the Cistercians from Burgundy, who fused manual labour with devotion. Implementing new farming techniques, the abbey became renowned for its large flock of sheep and wool exports, making it a centre of commerce and wealth. Religious life fused with the trade necessary to sustain devotional life and the survival of those dependant on the monks.

Victor first visited the abbey as a teenager when his parents moved from Glasgow to the Borders. Working for his Higher art, it became an old friend, a place to practise drawing and perspective, its South Transept window and door appearing on numerous sketch book pages. His art teacher, old Doddy Brown, had shown him a photo of Turner's painting of the abbey, and ever since the spirituality of the image had haunted him. Not in any Hollywood melodramatic fashion. What impressed Victor was the quality of light. And though not a churchgoer since his Sunday School days, Victor felt Turner had captured a promise in that light, as if the great window before which the tiny figure stood was the gate to heaven itself.

Melrose Abbey

Thirty years ago he brought Stella here. The gorgeous Stella with a mass of curled hair and green eyes emphasised by black eyeliner. On a day cosseted by May sunshine he'd asked her to fuse her life with his. 'To the end of time,' she'd promised. 'As long as these stones are here we'll be together.'

31

The stones remained, keepers of that earnest promise as of so many others, but Stella had returned to her native New Zealand taking their daughter Marielle with her. Marielle the tomboy. Always dressed in jeans and T-shirt, always climbing, scraping shins and breaking bones. Painting had been too static an occupation for her interest. Often Victor had tried to paint her, but found her mobile features and body difficult to capture satisfactorily. She was too wild a spirit to arrest in paint. Then she was gone, scraped from his canvas of existence. That was fourteen years ago and Victor hadn't seen either Stella or Marielle since. At first there were childish cards, occasionally a letter, even the odd phone call. Then nothing. His world had blown apart. Irresistibly, the abbey had drawn him back at that time.

The scarred abbey stones struck Victor as being keepers of the wisdom of the world. Their knowledge of humanity letting an aura of sympathy seep from their gritty surface, rise up from the supporting ground. Victor came to paint away his pain, to fuse it with the ancient, soothing stones, the tolerant ground, allowing them to comfort, returning his pain to him as their own brand of solace.

A new knot of curious gathered. One small boy pulled at his father's arm. 'That woman says there's a wizard.' His grubby hand waved vaguely. 'I wanna see the wizard,' he insisted. 'Come on.' Father looked at mother. Both shrugged.

A young woman, overhearing, explained, 'He means Michael Scott, the philosopher and mathematician. He dabbled in alchemy and the occult. He's thought to be buried here.'

'Oh, right. Thanks,' said the boy's father.

'See, I told you there was a wizard,' shouted the boy. 'I wanna see him.'

'He's not the sort of wizard that's in your Harry Potter books,' said his father.

The mother looked anxious. 'I could do with a cup of tea. Wouldn't you like an ice cream?' she asked her son.

Torn between wizard and ice cream he hesitated. His father grabbed his arm and dragged him swiftly towards the exit.

The painting was nearing conclusion. Victor touched in a few dabs of colour with a smaller brush, lifted a piece of card and with a final flourish swept an area of paint from the work, the only way he managed to come close to emulating Turner's painterly light. He stood back. It was finished. A murmured ripple swept round those watching, already turning away to sample the abbey's other attractions.

Victor felt drained. Exhausted. He always did after a painting session. People didn't realise it was such hard work. All they saw was the relatively short time spent before the easel. Usually an hour or two, though he sometimes painted a work in ten or fifteen minutes, as an event, often to raise money for charity. But he increasingly wondered if that was wise. It probably devalued his work. Time taken was equated with quality. He repeatedly reminded his audience of what Whistler maintained. That the length of time taken to produce a work was the result of forty years learning how to do it. The reaction of most was to ask who the hell Whistler was. Still, he couldn't blame them.

Slowly and methodically he started packing up his materials, wiping off his palette, knife, brushes, using kitchen roll and water from a plastic bottle. The sun had come through the clouds and he felt hot, wiping his brow with the back of his paint encrusted hand.

He became aware of a young woman at his side, scrutinising his painting. 'It's good,' she said. 'You're a good artist.'

Victor just nodded, continuing his packing up.

'I guess you've painted this scene plenty,' she said.

There was a twang in her voice but he couldn't place where she might be from. 'You on holiday?' he asked.

She smiled. 'You could say that.'

Victor, too exhausted to care whether he appeared rude, continued to pack his painting gear. He turned to remove the painting from the easel.

'How much?' she asked. 'How much for the painting?'

'That... rather depends.'

She laughed, a frank, life-embracing laugh, her unruly hair blowing across her face. 'You mean you fleece those who can well afford it?'

Despite his tiredness Victor smiled. 'Something like that.'

'Well, I'm not rich. Far from it. I'm working my way around the world, trying to earn money by painting.'

'You're from New Zealand, aren't you?'

'Yeah, but my father was from here. He used to paint the abbey, so my mother told me. That's why I'd like the painting. To remind me of

Note - J M W Turner had a long association with Sir Walter Scott. Turner was commissioned to illustrate Scott's books, and in 1831 visited the author at Abbotsford. After the author's death Turner also illustrated Lockhart's *Life*. Turner's watercolour *Melrose Abbey: Moonlight* was painted c1822.

Melrose Abbey

him and this place.'

Victor felt light headed, dizzy. Waves of heat washed over him, causing his heart to pound so much he wondered if he was having a heart attack. Steadying himself on the flimsy easel, he looked at her. Could she be...? Surely not. Yet why not? 'Your father... was he an artist?'

'Of sorts. My mother says he wasn't very good. He thought more of his work than anyone else did.'

'Oh!'

She smiled. 'Yeah, but that's all in the past. He died some time ago. We didn't come over. Mother said there was no point. He'd been a bit of a shit. He didn't bother keeping in touch. Apparently he'd no interest in me. Still, I'd like to have a painting to remind me of him. Of this place, which is special.'

'Yes, this place is special,' said Victor, his voice subdued. He picked up the painting, looking at it and then at the young woman. She didn't look like Stella. With a shock he realised she resembled him. But after what she'd said, he couldn't bring himself to tell her who he was. He was too tired for explanations. He knew he'd regret this moment for the rest of his life, but there it was. Another of life's disasters for the stones to console.

Turning to his bag he brought out a small brush, flicked the top from a tube of paint and dipped the brush into it. Leaning the painting on the easel he quickly signed the work. Vert. On the back he scrawled its name, *Fusion*. Past had fused with present. 'This work is priceless,' he said, a choke in his voice. 'Take it. I don't want payment. Just promise me you won't forget this day.' As she walked away in high glee, he said quietly, his fingers running over stones in the sun-warmed abbey wall, 'Goodbye Marielle.'

Fragments
by Lis Lee

I am a weaver, a spinner of tales,
hooking a verse with my fingers and nails.
I fabric a road winding low and high
to an ancient land beneath a bird-flecked sky.
I picture a river, the venerable Tweed,
wardened by heron, guard-sharp by the reed.
I steep-tread a ladder where salmon leap
and tryst with the thieving reiver, sleep,
to dream of legionnaries far from home,
who hold three hills in the name of Rome.
I dream while Cuthbert, saint to be,
Criss-crosses his holy way to the sea.
I dream while my countrymen loot and burn,
ruin castles and abbeys, turn by turn,
cut down the forests, sheep-seed the hills,
bank-side the river with chattering mills.
The titled and privileged feather their nests
in houses and castles with filigree crests,
while keepers shake their fists at birds of prey,
priming witless fowl for one glorious day.
Years pass as fast as the shuttles fly
and one more sparrowhawk slices the sky.
I am a weaver, knotting threads of time,
fringing my fabric with fragments of rhyme.

Heron in flight

35

The Cottage and the Ivy

By Lynne Henderson

'It's called Rosebriar Cottage,' someone once told me, when I asked. But I really don't know; there's no sign, no name on the map, no roses, no briars. It's always flickered in my vision when I've cycled past it, cruising along the narrow single track road, a Border byway, before I meet the next hill. I've never wanted to know anything else, the history, who lived there. It must be late nineteenth century, but the possible name and approximate age was enough for this ivy-clad ruin right by the road. Facts would shatter the spell. And sometimes I park my bike to explore, to clamber around it, when I'm in the mood, to mark the changes, to see what more time has done.

It's always been overgrown. Today, that's just the same. I start with the side that faces the road, a gable end of the cottage with a kind of byre attached. It nestles in the nettles and the rosebay willow herb, which protects the entrance to the byre with its magenta spears, while bustling bees busying themselves with nectar drone on and on. Standing outside the walls there's just the clamour of insects and me. The stillness I sense inside, through the barred door and windows, is suddenly assaulted by the furious thrashing of beating wings, and I tense as the shadows of roosting pigeons darken the sky. As the bees drone on, and the sun warms, the air becomes full – a heady blend of a sunny day's drowsy seduction, but it's laced with a drop of fear. And that's at the back of my mind. Do I really want to know what's inside?

Working my way round the edge of the building to the gable of the byre, I see that the ivy that once swaddled it in thick ruffles of green, has changed. I have noticed this before, it's the one change you can spot, even as you flicker past. What was once designer-draped in country cottage chic, not of climbing roses, but climbing ivy, has become a dead zone, blasted by chemical warfare. But now I see it close up. All the stems still cling to the random rubble, brown-grey gnarled and bony fingers reaching, twisting, entwining, the tortured skeletal remains of what once lived. Today it's quite dead.

As I round the cottage further, I have to climb over a gate that's meant to keep me out. But I tell myself I mean no harm. I'm in the field now and carefully stalk through the tall grasses to a window set at the back of the house but facing the road. There's a collapsed chaos of roof slates above. I move right in to the window, leaning against the stone stubbled with lichens, to peer through a promisingly sized gap between the nailed-up boards. I let my eyes adjust and wait.

What do we expect to see, I ask myself? Those of us that are attracted to abandoned places – not everyone is. What do we want to see?

Slowly I make out shapes: a small room, wooden shelving skirting the window area, more shelving further back, an old bottle standing, but I can't read the label. The larder I think, or small kitchen. It seems a safe start. But to the left I see an open door, which slants off into blackness. And on the door, stretched and hanging from an old nail with the weight of years in its folds, is a coat. It's some kind of over-all, frayed and thin on the seams and cuffs, heavily washed and heavily worn. And somehow, someone is suddenly there. Right there, just for a second. The someone who used to wear that coat, the someone who made it move, made it live. Perhaps they took a drink from that the bottle? Someone now dead and hanging from that hook. Maybe they took some poison from that bottle. Maybe they hung themselves. My mind runs on, all the clues are still there. If I could, I'd take the coat down. I shudder as I move away, stumbling over some branches hidden in the undergrowth like animal traps waiting to snap shut on living flesh and bone.

At last I'm standing outside the front of the cottage, which faces away from the road. It wouldn't have been right to make straight for it, far too presumptuous somehow, like marching uninvited through someone's front door. There's immediately a sense of privacy, safety from being out of sight and knowing this is the face of the house, basking in the sun, just a simple front door and one window either side. I look at the field area facing the door, where the garden would once have been. There's a dry stone wall long since brought to its knees by battling with thick trunks of ivy. There's no dogwood to link the cottage to its name. Maybe it was cleared long ago. There's nothing now. Maybe whoever lived here had a vegetable garden, frilled with cabbages and feathered with carrots. Maybe they harvested their own fruits to make jams and tarts. Perhaps they had a chicken coop, some pigs, a small holding for their survival, not just recreation. And the low murmurings of cows in the adjacent byre would have warmed and reassured them through their living room wall in the cold of winter as they struggled for a living.

After one more frantic flurry of escaping wings, there are no sounds. I'm alone with the boarded-up house. I find the only remaining means to see inside, just a chink through a window. A straggle of curling stems edge my view like a battered rococo frame. All I can make out is a stripped out interior, a chimney shaft and the curve of some steps leading upstairs, not much else. It seems disappointing.

But I have been inside before. Years ago, just once. And as I remember, lingering here in the heat outside, that once was enough.

Climbing through this very window, before it was finally closed off, I stood in the cool dimness with a sense of excitement, the excitement you have when you're a child exploring a place you're forbidden from entering. I carefully advanced, watching my step on a rotting floor yawning with gaps. Light entered through the blocked-up windows like torch beams slicing through floating dust motes, seeking life. And so was I.

There was an old piano, an upright, squeezed into a corner. I lifted the lid and there were the keys, the ivories yellowed and nibbled around the edges. I tried a few notes, very quietly, just teasing the poor thing. It didn't feel right and was so out of tune, so I closed the lid. But someone once played it, someone who may have sang songs. Maybe they played hymns on Sundays back then, maybe 'Auld Lang Syne' at New Year, the whole family crowded around the piano. Or maybe a young woman, a much loved daughter, played 'On the Banks of Allen Water', with a tear in her eye and an ache in her heart, feeling for the miller's lovely daughter in the song, who's pining for her soldier, but 'false was he'.

As I advanced to the stairway, past warped and wefted webs, the walls whispered no more voices. Maybe the coat on the back of that kitchen door tried to catch my arm to hold me back, I don't remember. Each gingerly placed creaking step I took, I felt the threat of the whole stairway crashing down. I still went up. Past faded sprigged chintz wallpaper rolling off the walls, revealing

Ivy on stone

flecked green paint layers underneath, walls imprinted with past generations, past identities, layer upon layer of time.

But when I got to the top, I wished I'd stayed out. I was standing in the main bedroom, its tiny attic windows open to the air. I was in the mind and heart of the house, where dreams are dreamt, plans are made, hopes are wished for. Looking around other people's houses has always been a nosy passion of mine. But I'd never seen a sight like it before.

Over the old bedstead frames was crawling a vast mass of ivy, advancing and piling into the whole room, finding its way in from the gable of the byre - no sign of this outside, but getting in nonetheless. I looked at the growing tips closest to me, just stray stems caressing at my feet, quite quaint, tiny tips of bright green gloss, soft and succulent. But further back the stems thickened, the leaves broadened, becoming darker and darker, tough, robust, determined. The ivy was taking hold, tightening and smothering, so you could hardly see anything any more. Its adventitious roots were embedded in the substrate of the heart of that house and it meant to blot out anything that lingered, to cut off and block out the light, to pull the house apart, to bring it down.

Turning aside to get out of the place, I noticed a dirty knitted rag doll crouched in a corner, but still with her button eyes, still wearing her pleated dress. I used to have a doll like that. Jemima was her name. I wondered what this doll was called. I picked her up and held her. I didn't want to leave her, but I didn't want to take her. So I took her downstairs and just before I left, I placed her sitting on the piano, in a sunbeam, so someone would find her, maybe take care of her, bring her back to life, or give her a decent burial.

So no, I never really wanted to go in that house again.

And today, I see why the ivy had to be killed off and all the windows barred, and I think of the ivy on my cottage wall at home, neatly trimmed for now, and I wonder. And just as I'm leaving this cottage, as I'm scraping past the side wall, I notice a single stem of green at the base, soft and succulent, clinging to a crack in the stone. And I realise. It's starting all over again.

Never Stopped Caring
by *Iona Carroll*

Ma name's Tommy Fair. Only I'm no that fair, not with the things I've done but I come from a fair toon, Kelsae.......... well, that's oor way of sayin it but the Sassenachs say Kelso, and that's their way. I've been gone a long time, twenty-four years it tis almost to the day......... and now I'm hame.

'Ye'll end in the gutter, Tommy Fair,' that's what they said to me in Kelsae. Ay. They were richt too. I've been around the world since leavin ma fair toon way back. Left when I was eighteen and many's the gutter I've been in since then. Been in bars an fights an seen the worst........... seen a man die in the streets once with a knife in his ribs. Had a woman in San Diego, she says to me, 'Look at your hand? You're always holding a glass! You're a drunk.'
I knocked her about a bit then. I'm not proud of that.

I mind in New Zealand it wis outside the People's Palace in Wellington........ I'd been on a bender for a week or more – this Salvation Army lassie says to me, 'Jesus loves you,' that was Claire, ye ken. They wis good for a meal an meant well, I guess. Anyways, Claire says this to me and she wis holdin one of them tins, ye ken the ones ye put the dosh in, 'Jesus loves you.' She said it twice, I mind.
Well, I grabbed her tin an threw it against the wall. Made a awfie clatter and a few coppers fell out onto the pavement. I mind that. 'Jesus disnae love Tommy Fair,' I yelled. 'Naebody loves Tommy Fair.' Then I thought of Nellie, she loved me, leastways she said she did, way back when she and me yaised to meet at the Abbey. I was drinkin even then...... could doon pints faster than any of me mates. Proud of that, I wis. More fool me.

'I dinnae want ye near ma dauchter, Fair,' says Nellie's father to me an he wis a muckle big man, wis in the Polis. I wis scared of him when I wis sober but took him on yin night after I'd had a skin fou. I thought Nellie loved me then. She wis scared of her Da too, that's why we met at the Abbey and that's why I left Kelsae, well........... I had to........ they all said I'd end up in the gutter, nae good for naebody. I widnae hiv been good for Nellie. I would hiv ruined her life. No decent woman would hiv had me – there's always been women....... but no one like Nellie.

I've been a hard man an seen many things in my life. Seen things since I left the Borders that's not fit for tellin but there's no a place on earth like the Borders an that's the truth of it. I'm gled I'm hame..... had to come hame to die..... like the elephants. Ye ken they go hame to die so they say. Well, I'm the same. Ay, the drink wis the end of me. They were all richt. The doacter in Embra gave me six month. It wis like a special announcement you get on Gala days. 'Mr Fair,' he says to me, not lookin me in the eye but up at the ceiling and clearin his throat in a funny sort of way, 'Mr Fair.....how can I put this to you?......I think it best if you were to put your affairs in order. I'm sorry.'

Sorry. He wisna sorry. The surgery wis full of folk waitin to see him and he wisnae for tellin them all to put their affairs in order!

Well, that's that, I thought. The end of Tommy Fair, born in Kelsae forty-two years ago....... soon to depart from Kelsae. I've no had a drop since the doacter telt me ma days are numbered an that was three weeks ago. Get yersel back to Kelsae, I thought, to the Abbey, to Nellie. Where is she noo? A grandmother nae doot.

But the Abbey would be the same though. Been there since 1128 so it's not for movin. Ye woudna think I know the date but I ken everything about the Abbey cause that's where Nellie and me yaised to meet. We'd lowp over the railings an go to our special place where the gravestones are set in the wall. Nae bather. It's a canny thing sittin here where me an Nellie yaised to sit lookin around at this braw place even if it's a ruin........ all thanks to the Earl of Hertford and Henry VIII – the English always wantin to destroy what wisnae theirs to destroy.

'You're good at History, Tommy,' Mr Anderson telt me. The only thing I wis good at. But I always had a head for dates. God knows where that came from? But I like being at the Abbey and looking at the stonework. It's a grand settin too on the Tweed. I've been everywhere but never seen anything to match it. You think I'm daft sayin that............. maybe it's because of Nellie.

I found a stone carving once, in the wall, of two heads.

'Take a look at this,' I said to Nellie and held her hand. 'This is ours...... oor special sign – Tommy and Nellie.'

'You daft ape,' she said but she stroked the heads too. Together we stroked the heads.

I'll look for the heads in a wee whilie but just want to sit a bit an think.

Ye ken..... I yaised to think there wis nae point in it all. Ye were born, suffered and died but now sittin here where me an Nellie yaised to sit, lookin up ....I wonder? Been thinkin of this place.....took them seventy-five years to build. Built stone by stone to the Glory of God. Men laboured here for God an they say God is love. All the work that love built now a ruin but ye ken, that's nae matter. Even if there wis nothin here, just a car park or a Tesco, it wouldn't matter at all because once Love built somethin here an that's the most important thing. That's the point. Nellie loved me but I wis afeard. That's why I ran away, not because of the drink but because I wis afeard of love. An Nellie knew. Women ken these things.

'Somethin's happenin to me? Jesus, I'm shakin all over. Hasnae been so bad this week. Christ. I'm scared. I cannae stop shakin. What's happenin to me?

I'm burnin up. The sweat's pourin off me!

Is there someone there? I thought I saw somethin. 'Is that you, Nellie?'

I'm on fire but I'm calm inside. God, I'm calm inside! What's happenin to me? Nellie..............?

'Jesus loves you, Tommy Fair.'

Kelso Abbey

Kelso Abbey

Lennel Kirk and Kirkyard
By Gwen Chessell

High above the River Tweed is a quiet place, where ancient yews stand like green pillars reaching for heaven. This place is approached by a path that winds steeply upwards across a thickly wooded slope. The path leads first to a grassy platform that looks out over the murmuring river below across to English farmland. A rough seat surrounded by brambles invites contemplation and, when the sun is shining, to some dallying to soak up grateful warmth. But something soon beckons the stranger to move on and wander over a simple stile set into a gap in a stone wall into a silent, sequestered place.

This is Lennel kirkyard, the resting place for hundreds of years of the folk of this area. It is a peaceful place, its other worldliness only interrupted now and again by the sound of a vehicle moving fast along the road that lies hidden from view on the other side of the opposite stone wall. Even birdsong is muted and respectful. Within this walled place, the air now hangs heavy and seemingly without warmth even when the sun illuminates the obelisks and pillars that mingle among the headstones. The silent, unchronicled stories of those who lie in the chill earth, earth that seems hardly ever touched by the sun's rays, hang suspended in that heavy air. 'I was here', the unspoken air cries out, 'I lived, I loved, I suffered, I saddened – how can I tell you my story?' Around the six feet of soil that hide the remains of the dead, the blurred stone monuments are the only remembrances of their passing; the only tangible hints that the dead lived at all. Perhaps seven hundred years of lives, from the most lowly to the highest in the land, seven hundred years of stories, now forgotten. But even in death, there is inequality. Some of high degree separated themselves from their more lowly brethren by their interment in another enclosure that is wreathed with rose and honeysuckle. But whether of high or low degree, in this, the oldest part of the kirkyard, most of the old graves lie untended; the inscriptions unreadable. Those who mourned each passing, have now passed on themselves and so the mourned become the unmourned.

And in the centre of the kirkyard, is the ancient kirk, now itself

Lennel Kirk and Kirkyard

decaying just as inevitably. Dark, aged yew trees give shelter to the shattered walls that still watch over the silent congregation. Unlike them, the kirk is still above the ground but ruinous and dilapidated. The north wall and the western gable stand, roofless but softened by a monstrous festoon of ivy. On the inside of the shoulder-high wall two monuments cling to the crumbling surface – one of pink granite and the other of white marble, their inscriptions so sharply crisp that they might well have been carved more recently but the two ministers they commemorate have been dead a very long time. The memorials hold locked within them the ghostly hint of sermons preached long ago, words now lost for ever. Outside this wall is a tall obelisk, crowned by a garlanded urn and with a dedication which is so decayed that only a name and a place are faintly discernible.

The kirk was hewn long ago from a local quarry. Its fallen stones are now green, moss-covered and in the summer, hidden under nettles and other rank plants. The kirk's benefice was linked to Coldstream Priory. Sir Walter Scott imagined Marmion, that noble villain, coming here, before the fatal day of Flodden. Perhaps he sought a blessing before that day that was to end for him, and for the Scots against whom he fought, so mercilessly unblessed.

Not all men respected those who had gone before them. At the east end of what was once the nave of the kirk, the existence of a mort-house testifies to those who did not scruple to use human remains as currency. In the days when anatomists were eager for cadavers to dissect, men kept watch here to keep safe the newly interred bodies of the dead. Now, the dark, dank interior of the mort-house is covered by a corrugated iron roof and the only living watcher is the occasional barn owl. Elsewhere iron bound mort-safes are pits for the unwary, sinking and decaying into the ground like their long mortified occupants.

But new life returns each spring, first when the snowdrops carpet the ground softening one's awareness of mortality and inevitable decay, followed by the joyful yellow of narcissi. In summer, the ground is covered by clover, vetch, nettles, blue geraniums, brambles and thistles. Insects hum and butterflies flit among the flowers. Not far from the kirk, another obelisk is obscured by four gigantic yews but through the yews, a determined rose has inserted itself and its orange-red hips hang brightly and defiantly against the blue-black berries of a bird-seeded mahonia. These interlopers are a welcome foil to the sombre green of the yew trees. The kirkyard gives its shelter to this day as burials still take place in the newer eastern end, and its existence continues to offer comfort and a place of contemplation to the newly bereaved. In this newer end of the kirkyard, lies a former prime minister, safely gathered in the soil of the country he loved best. This is still a place where the lives are celebrated, honoured and commemorated; the bereaved visit and remember. Life goes on.

Urban Degeneration
(Inspired by an abandoned factory in Hawick)
By Arthur Parsons

Fractured sockets stare at once proud cobbled streets,
Sightless but seeking echoes of the past
From the shuffling footsteps of the last local,
Still clinging to the tired terrace she calls home.

Soot-soiled stones tumble from factory gates
That once spewed flat-capped men and turbaned wives,
Rushing home to coal-stoked fires and pastry pies,
Hobnails hailing their escape to wives and mates.

The factory, now a girdered skeleton,
Whose bones complain to winter winds
Of gears and cables ripped and stripped from smashed machines
By mindless vandalism of time and man.

Oily-watered pools from broken pipes and drains
Distort the sky in rippled rainbow hues
And rust-red metalled sheets, like rosy cheeks,
Glow in the early evening heatless sun.

This rouged, corrugated face can only frown
Its heart and soul, a transplant in a foreign land.
The face no longer smiles or shouts a living sound.
Dead, with the postered epitaph, 'Redevelopment Planned'.

New History
By *Campbell Hutcheson*

Malcolm's cagoule was not waterproof. The evidence had begun to trickle down his back and dampen the waistband of his trousers. Putting chilled fingers in his pocket detected a tuna and mayonnaise sandwich in sponge form.

But at least the nine-year-old wasn't as miserable as the Roman centurion standing on the puddled stone platform. Microphone feedback failed to disguise the soldier's aside. 'God, last night...', he said, wiping a stubbly chin. 'Too early for me this.' Propped by an embossed metal shield, the armoured sentinel squinted at the onlookers sheltering in an umbrella forest. Mist obscured the Eildon Hills, dissolved the view of Roman Trimontium and obliterated the Scottish summer.

To Malcolm's father, the drizzle was a feature. A damp Melrose Festival was preferable to building sites. Two weeks' respite from belligerent contractors, faulty toilets and weak tea.

'Wait 'til you see the history,' Mr Fisher had said to his son.

'But I don't like history,' Malcolm said. 'Can't we go to the beach?'

His father was adamant that Malcolm, raised in Yorkshire, should learn more about his Borders descendants. 'We'll get to Coldingham,' he said. Malcolm imagined the Romans on Coldingham beach, playing volleyball and surfing. Sandals would be ideal.

Rejoining the coach, Malcolm doodled on the window condensation, glimpsing an impressionist's landscape through his wipings. Waving from a shiny veteran car, the Melrosian led the Tour of Ceremonies to Gattonside, the slumbering hamlet linked to Melrose by a chain bridge spanning the Tweed. In his youth, Mr Fisher had enjoyed causing the rickety walkway to bounce and tweak. It was guaranteed to make girls scream. Now cocooned in steel, the bridge's shoogling days were gone.

Several villagers, dressed as monks, mingled with tourists on the main street. 'Cherry?' said one, thrusting a wicker basket under Malcolm's nose. He accepted the burnished fruit and climbed the twisting path to the village hall. Inside, trestle tables groaned with sandwiches and home-baking. A small army of cheerful ladies fussed over the issuing of teas and coffees.

Watching tour followers flood into the hall, Mr Fisher said, 'I think we're going to be playing sardines. Let's try the garden.' Carrying plates and cups at head height, they squeezed between damp anoraks, raised elbows and matronly breasts to reach the rear exit. It was still raining. Umbrellas peppered the lawn and sheltered smiles.

'Do you want these?' said Malcolm, holding cucumber slices as if they were toxic waste. Mr Fisher accepted the offer as a large umbrella covered them.

'Ron? Ron Fisher?' said the brolly owner.

'Hey, Richard,' said Mr Fisher, unable to remember the man's surname. They shook hands.

'God, I haven't seen you in...'

'Fifteen years?'

'And the rest.'

As the two men drifted into schoolboy reminiscences, Malcolm watched children running around the garden. A black labrador sat panting beside its owner, a sturdy man wearing dark glasses and a pinstriped suit. The boy approached him.

'What's his name?' said Malcolm.

'He's a she, son. Flossie. I know, it's a stupid name. Blame my wife.'

Malcolm clapped the dog. 'Why are you wearing sunglasses? It's not sunny.'

The man smiled. 'It is where I'm standing.'

'That's not a Borders accent.'

'No, I'm from Yorkshire.'

'Really? Did army training in Catterick. Helluva place. Better than Afghanistan, mind.'

'Is that in Yorkshire?'

'No, well away from Yorkshire. Well away from Britain. Out of sight.'

Malcolm looked for the man's gun. 'Are you in the army now?'

'Not since last year. Retired. And Flossie's pleased about that. Aren't you, girl?'

Slowly, the umbrella parties dispersed and the cake-fuelled masses drifted like plastic ducks from the village hall. The veteran car's parp-parp was the signal for the procession to move off, cheered by a line of anoraked Gattonsiders.

'Dad,' said Malcolm. 'I need the toilet.'

Greener than an Irish theme bar, the manicured garden of Abbotsford House placed a protective arm around Sir Walter Scott's baronial home. Resident peacocks strutted between the bushes, their piercing calls warning intruders that they had no business spoiling the magisterial setting.

'I'll go behind that tree,' said Malcolm.

'You will not.'

'But I'm bursting.'

Mr Fisher looked around. 'Listen. While they're setting up the photo, just go through the front door. There's bound to be a toilet somewhere. Ask nicely, now.'

Malcolm scrunched over the stoned path as the photographer fussed and shuffled the festival group into pictorial order. The house's dark entrance and smell of old stone reminded Malcolm of a school trip to York. Peter Jenkins got lost (and was discovered testing the electronic doors of Tesco), while Barry Thompson made Rachel Smart kiss him in the Minster. 'Tasted of cheese and onion,' the pint-sized Lothario had told the back of the bus. It was Crispy Smart from that point. But she recovered, learning that the most effective response was kicking tormentors between the legs.

Unchallenged, Malcolm wandered along the dark corridor and discovered a small toilet, scented by yellow roses in a glass bowl. A clock chimed as he left, drawing him towards sunlight slashing through an open door. He poked his head around it. There were books shelved on three walls, almost floor to ceiling. Malcolm could barely read the titles on their gold-embossed covers, mostly brown, red and black. Even if he'd wanted to look at one, he couldn't. They were behind wire grilles and the shelving frames were locked.

Malcolm was still puzzling over the captive books when he returned to the entrance lobby.

'Quick,' said a woman, thrusting out a hand. She pinned a yellow rose to his cagoule and led him to the festive party in the forecourt.

'One more,' she shouted to the photographer. He hardly noticed, busy taking meter readings and girning at the sky. Malcolm's dad wasn't paying attention either.

Pointing a trumpet at Malcolm, a boy standing next to him said, 'You shouldn't be here.'

'I know,' said Malcolm. 'I should be in Coldingham. Smile.'

That did it. Malcolm couldn't get the beach out of his head. On returning to the coach, Mr Fisher noted his son's grumpy expression and folded arms. 'Look, the rain's going off and we're nearly back in Melrose,' he said. 'Half an hour, tops.' The thunder cloud above Malcolm's head did not shift. 'Hey, what's the problem, chief?'

'Nothing... apart from all this being so old,' said Malcolm.

'Old?' said Mr Fisher, unzipping his jacket. 'That's what you call history. Part of my culture, part of your culture. Forget about the weather. This is a celebration and it's only once a year. You'll remember today.'

'Can't we see new history?' said Malcolm.

'Okay, okay,' said his father. 'Something more recent. Eh, let's try Tweedbank. We can slip over when the coach stops at Darnick. It's not far.'

Father and son sauntered past small white houses, decorated with postage stamp lawns. The excited voices of children tumbled from driveways strewn with cycles, tennis racquets and toy prams. Tethered to a drainpipe, a fat alsatian barked towards the squeals. The winding street ended abruptly, tarmac crumbling into a gravel and dirt path. Gnarled trees, impenetrable bushes and foot-high grass lay ahead of the searchers.

'We'll need to spread out,' Mr Fisher said.

'But what are we looking for?' said Malcolm. His father winked and tapped the side of his nose.

Malcolm broke off a large twig from a tree and whacked the grass as he walked. That would chase off snakes. But he found nothing, apart from damp soil, weeds and dog mess. Just as he turned to check on his father's progress, Malcolm's sandal clipped a heavy object. The rusting metal bar protruding from the soil appeared to be fixed to concrete. It carried no markings. Was it upside down? Malcolm ran his finger along the bar, lifting fine brown powder from the bubbled surface.

'Bingo,' said Mr Fisher. 'You've found it. Any idea what it is?'

His son shrugged.

'It's a railway line,' said Mr Fisher. 'Part of the Waverley Route. This was the Borders junction in 2014.'

'That's years ago,' said Malcolm. 'Why is it not marked?'

'Son, not all history is remembered,' said his father.

Hume Castle and Rhymers Tower
By Dougie Morrison

The very term Scottish Borders gives reason for the many ruined castles, keeps and abbeys. Always at the forefront of wars, battles and skirmishes with our English neighbours. But it was not always the English who were a threat. In 1313, Robert the Bruce, King of Scots, embarked on a scorched earth policy and destroyed all the castles in the Borders to try to ensure the English could not retake them and gain strongholds once more. Hume Castle, near Kelso, known as the Eyes of the Borders, is the only one he did not destroy, for some reason. Perhaps he thought The Merse (marshland) was defence enough to prevent English occupation, but this marshland even hindered the Scots at the Battle of Halidon Hill, or maybe he thought he had to keep it as a warning beacon to alert him of an invasion.

It survived until Colonel Fenwick on behalf of Oliver Cromwell bombarded it with artillery and reduced it to ruins in 1651. It must have been terrifying living in the borders until after the merging of the English and Scottish parliaments in 1707. It is an example of one of the earliest types of castle in Scotland more often found in the West Highlands. In 1460 King James II was killed by cannon which exploded when he was trying to set the fuse.

The castle was captured and retaken several times. When you go to the ramparts it is easy to see why it was built there. There is an excellent 360 degree view and you can see for miles in every direction due to being 373 feet above sea level. In the centre a tower once stood which would have acted like the crow's nest on a ship, I presume, although it has been destroyed to render it below its original height. Nearby there is a well that would slake the defenders' thirst. It has seen many battles in the surrounding countryside, mainly on the Cheviot Hills side.

In 1804 it was used as a beacon station during the Napoleonic Wars. It has been visited by Mary Queen of Scots and James IV too. On January 31st 1804 a sergeant of the Berwickshire Volunteers mistook charcoal burner fires on Dirlington Law for a warning and lit his beacon at the castle and set in train the lighting of all the Border beacons to the west and there was a turnout of 3,000. As I stood looking over the vista I could hear voices from a farm some distance away. It is not huge and there did not appear to be to be signs of any real living quarters. Sprouting freely in one corner were two thistles as if to declare this is a Scottish landmark and outside on a down sloping hill there was an army of thistles leading to a stout tree which I can imagine dangled many an enemy who had been captured. The outside is taller than the inside and I suspect that if the archaeologists moved in they would find relics of a bygone and violent age.

In 1789 the castle walls were reconstructed in their present form and the original 13th century portions are still visible in part.

The most fascinating ruin for me, however, is Rhymer's Tower in Earlston. Thomas Learmont was the landowner who was born and lived in the castle. He was known as True Thomas or more familiarly as Thomas the Rhymer. Earlston was then known as Ercildoune. Born in the 1200s, the legend is that he was mysteriously abducted on the east side of the Eildon Hills by the Queen of the Fairies and taken to Elfland as her lover. When he returned seven years later, he was unable to tell a lie and had the gift of prophesy.

Among his predictions was the death of King Alexander III, the night before he fell off his horse and died, The Battle of Bannockburn (1314) after which the Scottish Nobles had to sign The treaty of Arbroath to swear allegiance to King Robert the Bruce. This document is thought to be the basis of the American Constitution. He also predicted the defeat of the Scots at Flodden in 1513 which is still commemorated to this day on the Selkirk Common Riding, and the Union of the Crowns which thankfully eventually let us live in peaceful co-existence with each other. It was said that he had greater powers than Merlin, so I think the Scottish King missed a trick there! The Rhymer was said to live for another seven years before the Queen of the Fairies sent her hart and hound to fetch him back to the Land of the Elves forever.

Rhymer's tower has a wonderful little cafe adjacent today, and if you go downstairs, you can enjoy excellent food or a coffee beside the proprietor's garden pond. There are Koi Carp swimming leisurely just beneath the only standing wall and references are visible of the Myth of True Thomas.

So strong is the legend, that if you are in the reception of the Borders General Hospital you can see the wonderful mural by Alasdair Macleod painted in 1988, showing an abridged story of the Rhymers tale.

Go to the ruin and let your imagination run free while you enjoy a latte!

A quest in the ruins of time

By Russell Bruce

Gwilliam watched Avelise butter her toast. He never tired of watching her.

Her mobile rang. Her eyebrows narrowed, dimming the perpetual smile in her eyes. 'I'm coming.' She closed the mobile. 'It's Liam,' she said.

Gwilliam nodded and handed her his car keys.

'I'll be with you in spirit on the last leg,' Avelise said as they kissed.

Leaving the hotel at Carfraemill, Gwilliam strode steadily out on this last leg of the walk from Melrose to Soutra following the old Girthgate or Via Regia . They had intended camping last night but the heavens had opened and they'd spent the night at the Carfraemill Hotel south of Oxton.

He was surprised to find he was looking forward to doing this last section on his own. Something inside him was saying linger, stop, listen on this last stage of a latter-day pilgrimage through time.

He had come Scotland to do a postgraduate degree in environmental history at Edinburgh and met Avelise one evening when out walking on Salisbury Crags. Nearing the end of her medicine degree, Avelise was half French, half Scottish. Gwilliam had come to feel he was too but his parents were quite definitely both French. His mother came from Normandy and his father from Marseille.

He and Avelise had been together for almost a year. The fusion of bodies was also a fusion of minds. Neither were believers but if they did have something akin to a soul those would be fused too. It was as if they'd known each other from the beginning of time.

He'd reached Oxton now and was heading north on the old route out of the village. Strange, he'd meant to leave the car at Falla yesterday ready to pick up at the end of the walk but drove on and left it at Carfraemill, catching a bus and walking the last stretch to join Avelise at Melrose. That had made it easy for her this morning to get back to Melrose to go to Liam. Perhaps what had been an absentminded mistake might pass for prescient thoughtfulness.

As he approached the Roman Camp he imagined the beat of legionnaires feet travelling north. Ordered. Disciplined.

But something changed. The sound of voices. The mixture of tongues that came with Roman legions recruited or dragooned from across the Empire. These were stragglers on the retreat. They'd be gone soon. Gwillian stretched his aching limbs. Scotland was a lost cause for the Roman Empire. He longed for Gaul.

A legionnaire was chasing a young woman who found herself in the wrong place at the wrong time. He was struck by her flowing red hair and moved towards them to intervene. Her attacker launched at her ankles.

She seemed to fall almost in slow motion and with such grace. Then leveraging her body upwards she rose whilst turning with incredible speed as her attacker lunged again. A knife glinted in an arc and the leveraging arm locked on to the other elbow propelling the blade with lightning force. He dropped to his knees. An open neck stared in blind and petrified astonishment.

She stood over him but a second. And was gone.

Gwiiliam followed.

Gwilliam walked on, serried patches of conifers replaced the birch copses and solitary rowans already bunched with the fruit of summer. He thought of Avelise and Liam. Warm and thirsty he'd stop by the valley that traversed his route before the rest of the climb. There was no hurry.

Closing his eyes he thought about the Augustine Monastery that was his objective. The monks had perfected an ancient recipe. A draught ensured surgery and even amputations could be carried out whilst the injured or gangrenous were in a deep and pain free state of unconsciousness. So sophisticated were they that it was thought they established the amount to be administered depending on size, weight and physical strength of the patient.

Gwilliam's task was to learn and record their knowledge and achievements. He would need to make a move and as he roused himself he found he was looking into the eyes of a young woman with flowing red tresses and deep soft green eyes.

'I know why you've come and I can help you,' she said.

They travelled on together. She spoke French, Latin and Hebrew and knew a language of the north, but soon the sky was darkening as the sun sank and they prepared for the night. Gwilliam lit a small fire and

*cooked a simple meal, grinding juniper berries on a stone to flavour
a piece of the boar belly bought from a hunter further south. Avelise
collected burdock leaves and roots to cook over the fire.*

*In the morning she was gone. Only the crushed bed of grasses beside
him to mark where she had lain.*

The white swishing blades marked time, driven ratchet wheels
of endlessness powering homes beyond these hills. They stand
between the new road and this old road, Dere Street, Malcolmes
Road, Via Regia, Girthgate. Much of it following the same line as
the Roman road but with name changes reflecting the different
periods of usage. It seemed all history had passed through; armies,
kings, queens, monks, merchants, packmen, thieves, vagabonds
and spies.

From the top, the rest of Scotland lies before you. Behind links to
all of Europe. A highway of the past, buildings camps and events
saturated the time and weather razed land.

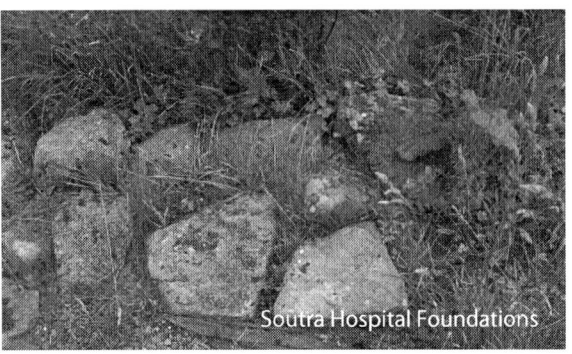
Soutra Hospital Foundations

Monks of the old Celtic church travelled south to evangelise
England. Perhaps a Scotic church and a brotherhood of Culdees,
Céli Dé, preceded the St Augustine monastery on the hill. The care
of the poor and sick would have been a natural communion of ideals
and purpose as Benedictine and Augustine influence travelled
north replacing the older church of Columcille.

Armies from the south or north passed each other in time to
return victorious or defeated. Blood soaked into a ravenous earth.

*Gwilliam looked up. A soft rustle in the birch copse alerted him to
her presence.*

56

'What are you cooking for me today?' she asked.

'And what have you brought to our table?' asked Gwilliam.

'Fresh spring water, pressed cream cheese and something very special.'

Avelise's eyes dropped slowly the length of her body and Gwilliam saw the child nestling into her skirts, the familiar soft red hair and shy green eyes.

'You have a daughter,' Gwilliam said.

'As have you, Gwilliam,' Avelise smiled.

The child came towards him where he sat cross-legged in front of his fire cooking the morning-caught trout wrapped in sheaves of sorrel. Gwilliam turned. The child gently touched his arm, tiny fingers reaching up for his face. Gwilliam closed his eyes, waves of paternal feeling coursed through his veins like a tsunami. Were those tears seeping through his eyelids like the final release of the grapes?

He stretched out his arms and opened his eyes again. He was on his own.

Picking up his rucksack Gwilliam headed off towards the site of the old Resting Place where the stones of a medieval inn rose in curving truncated stumps on the open hill. As he drew near the sky grew dark and the landscape took back its older form.

Rank grass gave way to upland meadow. Splattered white dots of sheep melted. Groups of grazing, hardy black cattle munched contentedly on this plateau of summer goodness. The air thick with the smell of meadowsweet.

It was unusually crowded, travelling monks, old women selling the meagre produce of the land, others with baskets of fresh herring from the coast for the monastery.

Avelise flowed through the crowd.

A stranger watched her in awe. 'Best keppit yer een and thochts stranger,' a monk said quietly.

Avelise knelt down by a seated figure leaning against the stone wall. He'd been a big man, but by his bleached leather pallor this was the old man's his last journey.

Now on his feet, Avelise held her arm round Liam's waist and her daughter, now perhaps about ten, held his hand as they walked north again through a sun-spattered mist. They'd be safe at the monastery.

Gwilliam joined the monk. He knew Edward's army, proud, disciplined and determined was not far away and he needed to find out about numbers, morale, horses and the state of their supplies. He was sure Edward was heading towards Stirling. Edward II was determined to stamp his authority and superiority over Scotland and finish his father's work once and for all. His troops outnumbered three to one Bruce's army. This ground would be trampled by thousands of feet, the largest English army ever to invade Scotland. The less they found of use to them the better. More blood for the ravenous soil.

Gwilliam could now see Soutra Aisle as he walked the last few hundred yards over land which had drawn into itself the long gone monastery and hospital of Soutra. Soutra Aisle was built later with the stones from the old monastery as a chapel and finally used as a mausoleum for local lairds.

Avelise was waiting for him. 'Liam's gone,' she said. Gwilliam nodded and held her. He knew just how much her grandfather had meant to her.

Two weeks later Gwilliam and Avelise are in a tiny flat in the Ile de la Cité where the Seine splits round these ancient islands in central Paris. Liam has left her the little Paris flat. All that remained of the family's old French estates. Gwilliam is cooking a lobster bought in the market that morning Avelise opens a bottle of champagne.

'To Liam,' they chorus, clinking glasses.

Later after they have eaten, Avelise walks over to the corner of the main room. Shelves stacked from floor to ceiling with books in a dozen languages. On the floor is a small kist dark with age. She opens the lid and carefully pulls out a vellum manuscript.

'I promised to get a copy of this for you a very long time ago, and Liam asked me to give you the original,' said Avelise.

Gwilliam takes the book with its darkened, battered pages and irregular torn edges. He gently prizes it open. Gwilliam is entranced by these stained and watermarked vellum pages with neat columns of writing in ancient hands.

He was not a student of medieval manuscripts but he knew something about the preparations of the skins for the vellum. Scraped of flesh and hair, soaked in lime solution, and scraped again, the rotting leather slippery and floppy. Yet more washing

Soutra Aisle

and scraping followed by stretching and scraping. Finally, drying and still more scraping until a writing material that could last a thousand years was ready for sewing and the pens of scribes.

Gwilliam understands the significance of this manuscript. It was from the long lost library of Soutra.

It recorded the mix of herbs and extracts the monks used to prepare the draught to ensure patients would feel nothing of the operations they faced. Details of the judgements made for individual patients, the successes and failures, how long the patient remained in a state of unconsciousness and surprisingly often names, all intended to guide those who would use these medieval methods of surgical preparation in future.

'It was a dangerous manuscript if it found its way into the wrong hands,' explains Avelise. 'In the mid fifteenth century when corruption and mismanagement of Soutra's vast estates was taking place, the library and scriptorium at Soutra also fell into disarray and this manuscript was rescued and eventually brought to France. It has survived, in secret, over the centuries whilst the remainder of Soutra's medieval medical library, early Christian texts and stories of Celtic folklore were dissipated in the winds of time.'

On a Scottish hillside Liam's ashes blow in those winds of time, smiling as they birl in the evening breeze.

Footnote - A charter dating from c1220 states that a pound of pepper and another of cumin were to be rendered annually by the master of Soltre (Soutra) for the tithes of Fulwithnes in the parish of Channelkirk, indicating that Soutra bought spices and herbs from around the globe apart from the opium seeds and hemlock used in the anaesthetic draught.

At Hadrian's Wall
By Julian Colton

Eponymously named, it's certain I came.
Not an anoraked tourist, greedy archaeologist
seeking buried treasure, power by osmosis,
this pathetic need to possess
hoarded artefact and secreted knowledge.

Like time-lapsed, grassed over ruins show,
walls can be more concept than reality,
chains of command often tenuous.
Though why dwell on failings and mortality?
With my desire to educate and civilise,
to shut out barbarous Northern tribes,
I truly convey the emblems for posterity.

As omniscience was beyond my imagination,
rule became a question of organisation:
ability to lay bricks and mortar,
install central heating and running water,
at peace, keep the legion's muscles supple,
permit my architectural dreams to flourish.

To be greater than a bureaucrat's tool
– the guy who yawns and stamps the seals –
I marched with my men, ate their meals,
sang their songs, slept in their quarters.
I knew what I was doing, I was no man's fool.

Between pressing the flesh and affairs of state
these fine robes not mere presentation.
Speeches at the senate weren't always ghost-written.
At home, I commanded proper respect,
patronised the arts, allowed commerce to thrive
blew the flames of Empire alive.

Despite my love for the youthful Antinous
– dig deep, find his lovely, ravaged bust –
Hadrian – adopted Spanish son of Trajan
becoming of the name Caesar to all Romans.

But its empty, far-off windswept places
– Caledonia, Danube and Euphrates –
margins sleeping citizens never see
that secured a sense of Rome, history and me.

A wall creates – and breaks –endless possibilities.

At Hadrian's Wall first appeared in The Eildon Tree, issue 12 Summer 2005 and in
Two Che Guevaras 2007.

Moss covered walls

The Keeper of the Castle
By Chris Fairgrieve

Unable to sleep, early on a surreal, subtle summer morning, with the sky lightening in the East and driven by late night insomnia the young man left the house, out of the warm fire-glow, out into the stillness, closing the front door behind him. He regarded the moon and breathed lungfuls of the still clear air as he made his way out across the fields heading for the old castle perched on top of the hill. The familiar route seemed different in the early morning and the morning had a particular sense of peace about it which descended all around. On the horizon, the hills of the border lay silent save for the drifting call of a greylag goose moving above the mantle of herringbone cloud. Down the valley a roe buck barked a warning, declaring its territory and the sound only accentuated the timeless feeling that the morning conveyed as if he had left behind one world and was moving slowly back into another, more primeval universe.

He walked slowly and purposefully with his senses fully awake, softened only slightly by the after effects of the pills he had taken in the nightclub several hours ago. In his ears, the ringing gradually lessened and the noisy vocals, bass lines and rhythms of the dance music floated away into the silence. It had been a good night of carousing and now still wide awake he allowed his mind to relax, enjoying the isolation and feeling as if he was the only person in the world for a brief moment. As he approached the castle mound a string of jackdaws rose from inside the walls, breaking the silence with their calls and wing beats and his heart raced as he scrambled up through the damp grass, onto the great stone steps and climbed up to get a better view.

As he stood on the parapet looking out over the patchwork of fields, trees and smallholdings he surveyed the landscape with a satisfied feeling and a warm glow in his belly. Not a soul was stirring across the land and he felt the timelessness of the surroundings slowly come to his mind, thoughts wandering among the battles, history and ancient tales of the Borderlands.

Just then, as he closed his eyes and savoured the moment, he was startled by a cough from down below within a corner of the castle and turned with surprise to see a figure there, tending a fire and singing softly to himself. After the initial feeling of annoyance that his reverie had been disturbed by someone else, he felt a mixture of trepidation and curiosity at the strange man who appeared to have made the castle his home for the night. On the ground beside the fire lay a bundle and a stout stick made of hazel, a blanket spread out as if the man tending the fire also could not sleep and was savouring the early morning atmosphere.

'Hallo,' the old man called to him in a gentle voice which carried through the air as if from another time and place and for a startling moment made him think that the figure had been expecting him. He was bearded, much older than the young man and he seemed relaxed, waving a hand towards the young man, beckoning him to come over and join him by the fire. The young man regarded the figure, dressed simply in what looked like old clothes, antique clothes in fact, as he stooped over the fire and placed more branches on the flames from a pile of wood stacked in the corner of the castle. A vagrant perhaps, stopping for the night on his way through the countryside, but he also seemed like he was part of the scenery, part of the living breathing castle and the young man approached him nervously.

'Hello there,' he greeted the vagrant from a few steps distance, appreciating the warmth of the fire and wondering whether he should be so bold as to shake his hand.

'Strange to be meeting another soul so late at night,' the old man ventured, 'but come and join me by the fire. The company will give me great pleasure and conversation likewise.'

'Passing through are you?' he asked. 'Or do you live locally?'

'Bit of both really,' the old man replied, 'my people have been here for centuries but we're always on the move. I've been away for a time, but tonight I have my fire to tend, part of a pilgrimage I make to this place, ancient history you could say. Let me explain. I am a wanderer, physically and in spirit, and make my fire as a precaution, a beacon ready to signal against invaders, not for warmth or companionship. And tonight is special you see, it's been many years since I have returned here but look over there and you'll see another like me, ready to signal too if I build my beacon high enough, to give warning of the advancing army.'

Advancing army? Beacon against invaders? The young man

looked to the West and in the distance indeed could make out the outline of a ruined tower, smoke gently rising from it through the skyline. The young man's mind raced, here was a character right enough, a bit of an eccentric at best, insane at worst. It was hundreds of years since there had been armies and battles in this particular castle. However, something about the honest way he spoke and his open manner made him seem credible.

'So you've been away from here, now you're building your fire, tell me your story, where have you been?' He asked, trying not to let the sarcasm show in his voice.

'Sit then awhile, on this blanket of mine and I will tell you.' 'Once I was born into and lived in a noble house, a castle grand with many inhabitants, great hunting hounds and fine ladies. I was taught in peaceful times by wise men, and my own father, in all the great disciplines, grew up a fine young man with all the opportunities of the world at my feet. That made the place I had grown up somehow inadequate to me, lacking in challenges for my vain intellect. Everyone knew I was destined for greater things. So they sent me away.'

'Where did they send you?'

'First of all I sailed to the colonies, to see the great forests, find out how the rest of the world lived and come back to tell them of what I had seen. That made me restless and unable to adjust to life. After what I saw believe me you look on your own home in a whole new different light. Imagine countries where it rains daily half the year, real rain mind, and the world is green, huge and green, in the forests and in the fields. I saw weird and wonderful creatures, walked with elephants and marvelled at the primates I soon learned were our cousins. Our domain was the forest, and all its wonders. We walked through its dense life led by the ones who live there and recorded all we could to tell of what we had seen. You will know of what I speak now that they have shown it here on television. But television cannot convey the entire way of life that those people live. There is darkness too in their lives, no paradise or garden of Eden.'

'Thereafter I wandered North out of the great swathes of forest and came upon another ancient people and followed them in their great migrations herding cattle in search of grazing and water. These people worshipped their cattle and showed me another

Hume Castle

way of life I had never seen before, a proud warrior race who never stayed long in any one location and taught me how to live as a nomad.'

'Then I returned and lived on the European continent, still seeking to solve all the questions in my mind at that time, in winters that were cold and summers mercurial. There I fell for a woman and gave up my life to her, but when once we had loved after some time we were in love no more and I became a broken man. I returned to these shores to find my people all dead and buried.'

'What had happened to them?'

'They had perished at the hand of the invaders from there,' he pointed South, to England, 'all of them put to the sword and our great home burnt to the ground. The ruins you see here are all that is left of that home.'

'So what did you do then?'

'What indeed. Thoughts of revenge filled my mind for years and I struggled with those inner demons until my whole body ached but there was no way alone I could avenge their deaths. I was also peaceable by nature and though many might think me coward I railed at the thought of more violence. Instead I became a wanderer to this day, making my way by telling the stories of the life I had led and relying on the kindness of those who heard my tales. So for all these years I have lived a simple life far from the past of which I have told. I would take myself away to foreign lands once more but then who would return to tend the fire here in case of the attack which may surely come?'

'So that's why you've ended up here tonight and lit this fire?'

'Yes, and as we speak I must collect more wood to have at hand, ready for the fire to be stoked high and send my signal if necessary. I am going down to the valley where there is firewood. May I ask if you would wait here by the fire until I return and we can talk some more?'

The old man gathered up a length of rope from his bundle to tie up more firewood and walked out of the castle entrance, down the grassy mound and started making his way slowly into the valley below, heading towards a small cluster of trees. The young man climbed up onto the parapet once more and watched him disappear among the trees, fading from view as he went, like an apparition, disappearing into the dawn light among the trees. Then he returned to the fire and lay down on his side to rest and wait for the return of the strange old man.

Hours later he awoke from a deep sleep in the bright sunlight of midday, with the embers of the dwindling fire still glowing but no sign of the old man. The bundle, hazel stick and blanket were gone and not a trace remained of any other human being. Rubbing the sleep from his eyes, all of a sudden he had the strangest feeling that he had met with something supernatural and with this thought he rose up, goose-pimples tingling on his skin, and set off for home. The gentle breathing of the wind through the pine trees rose up to the castle walls and he let his gaze linger on the valley below and wondered if the old man had been real or if he would ever return.

Forest Ruins
By Carol Norris

The ancient Caledonian Forest once covered most of the Borders, we know that. However it does not lie in ruins before our eyes – its ruin is not seen, rather it is only by absence now that its loss may be known. That is apart from the faint residual traces that can be found or imagined to be here and thereabout. We live by such a trace, fringed by a remnant of the ancient forest to the North. Nevertheless, this remnant still has energy enough left to tumble down into the glen, the bed of the burn that runs past our bedroom, lulling us to sleep every night with its gentle music. An ancient stump of this forest recently came to light. Buried invisible beneath the burn for years and years, it came to light only after a torrential flood tore down the glen, excavating and deepening the bed by over two feet and revealing what at first appeared to be rock, and may well be a partly fossilised tree, but definitely was at one time wood.

In this remnant of ancient forest there are still many wild cherry trees, the blossom of which, in May, carried high above in the canopy, appears like a fresh fall of snow covering everything. Then there is the gale resistant Yew, whose sinewy roots connect with all other Yews throughout the land, who commune with each other and remember for a very long time, for eons of time. The yew is called The Tree of Death for its poison, and nothing will grow under a Yew, everything withers and dies, but it is also the Tree of Life for its Taxol, from the bark and the fresh leaves, powerful against cancers, known in Nepal thousands of years ago and now re- remembered by science.

Crab apple trees, oaks, hawthorn, elders, rowan and Scotch pine complete the complement of trees, hallmarks of the ancient Forest of Caledonia. Snowdrops come, then soon following, oceans of narcissi, bluebells later. Then come forget-me-nots, columbine, named after St. Columba, a Latin name meaning dove, because this flower resembles a dove in flight, honeysuckle, whose sweet scent can carry more than a hundred miles to those in certain transcendant and receptive states, and lilies of the valley, who keep their perfume hushed and hooded close to.

Birds that visit us include thrushes, Siberian thrushes, still wearing the Hammer and Sickle under their wings, the Goldfinch, Greenfinch and Siskin, the Greater Spotted Woodpecker with vermilion flashes, the Nuthatch, the Tree creeper, the Dipper, flitting like a shadow up the burn and then walking under water, the Heron, the glorious Technicolor Pheasant, who came to stay. He was named The Reverend after his perfect, circular white neck collar and pompous demeanour, which was soon changed to Bully Bird after his treatment of male rivals. There is also the beautiful Yellow Wagtail, faithfully waiting for his mate the winter through, fascinated by what he sees as the endless re-appearances of her in every window, and especially the car wing mirrors, which became an almost constant perch.

One day, alas, a mass of yellow and grey downy feathers appeared on the frosty grass, all that remained of the wagtail, presumed victim of severe cold and scavengers, never to be seen again. That is until two weeks later, Easter morning, when a pair of wagtails were seen dancing on the kitchen windowsill. A joyful day. Every March, a pair of Mallard ducks from the nearby River Tweed, make daily repeat visits to inspect our small burn and tiny pond. Motionless, they study the environs while appearing to be lost in a ritual of contemplation. They commune with each other to ascertain whether the site is suitable for their nursery requirements. This year for the first time after many years of this process, wonderfully, they decided it was. Eight beautiful baby ducklings were proudly brought out to be admired. There then followed a period of intense anxiety for us, dive bombing crows who came too near them and making urgent forays onto the adjacent busy main road sometimes inevitably, due to the most pressing circumstances, regardless of the state of undress one was in, to halt traffic when one, perhaps two, of these balls of mobile fluff escaped parental supervision and careered onto this busy road. One day they all vanished together with mother, having been launched into the burn with intent and whizzed down the half mile to the Tweed. We were relieved and could at last relax, less obsessed by the proximity of birds of prey.

We are surveyed by high overhead Buzzards and Red Kites effortlessly circling on the thermals, an occasional swooping visit by a Hawk to more closely inspect our visitors and the Owl provides our night time mood music.

All the Tit family are permanent residents, including the Long

Borders woodland

Tailed variety who live up the glen and of course Robin Redbreast. Tiny, quiet, brown Jenny Wren lives here, who despite tremendous shyness has the most bold and beautiful song.

We have resident animals; squirrels, moles, tiny voles with lovely black eyes who easily become all of a tremble, stoats and weasels who have the prettiest faces, not to their prey I suppose. They love playing amazing games. Travellers up the burn include Mr. Otter, in transit from the Tweed, probably nightly, but we have only seen him once, and Mr. Badger who visited once, in great power, to up heave and eat a giant wasps nest leaving a hole three feet deep and four feet across.

Passing like a ghost, silently through the greenwood, from time to time, comes the Roe deer, always alone, or with calf, the Changeshaper, Spirit of St. Patrick, it is said.

A Salmon once came down the burn, from where nobody knew. But then, you see, there is a greater mystery than this; no one knows how the water in our burn flows down at all since its source, a loch, is lower than the head of our burn and everybody knows that water cannot flow uphill.

Perhaps the ancient trees are not all completely ruined, completely lost after all – perhaps their roots are still lifting water to the sky.

Not new, but it'll do!

By Jane Houston Green

High up on the longer wall there is a stone, rather curious in shape, surrounded and protected by others in the area slightly to the left above the window opening. It might take a while to locate this particular stone but eventually you will decide which is me, and when you do, I have to apologise for not waving or smiling but that is hardly in either my nature or range of abilities. Old Rab placed me here with his strong, gnarled hands many a year ago and when he did so he whispered some special words that spoke to the eternity buried deep inside the grains and fragments of my essential being. 'Always be filled with a pleasant cheer as ye settle here from year tae year.' Now Rab was hardly a memorable poet but when it came to being a dry stone dyker and stone mason he was a master surpassed by none. Nearly eight hundred years have passed now and while some parts of this modest, yet perfectly formed stone tower, have not stood the test of time my section still stands proudly surveying a landscape that has, nonetheless, changed a little since that May in 1258. Or was it October? It must have been the May as I remember having the sun warm me for many an hour for a few months and that would mean the longer days of summer. Much less damaging than that lethal combination of frost, ice and snow ... not good for buildings really but all part of the seasons, I suppose. What was it I heard the other day? There is always a price to pay for everything, and sure enough the way a year evolves gives it a movement and energy that is pleasing to experience, so I have learnt to survive the bitter winter winds and howling gales.

Now you may be wondering why this place was actually built and that question has been pondered by many as they have trampled through the undergrowth, stumbled on fallen stones and measured from one corner to another before disappearing off to some point yonder and beyond. History likes to presume and archaeology moves to correct but whatever the actual truth my great purpose in life was to help provide a home for Thomas Learmont and his entourage of family, friends, and occasional envious foe. Not that the latter stayed around long as Thomas was a perceptive, commanding man who could make others uneasy with the twitch of a finger or arch of an eyebrow. At that time the surrounding area was called Ercildoune and the present village of Earlston simply did not exist. Perhaps you need a minute to imagine this ... try to take away everything that is here. Clear the site, and sight, so to speak. Now that should leave you with very little apart from the essential river and numerous oak trees but now we must add this tower in all its former glory, a few stone huts with thatched roofs and in the distance a church where the sound of monks singing carries on the wind as it whispers down the valley. When this picture has clarified in your mind then it will be easier to understand the domain that existed for Thomas, a Scottish laird, known for a few quirks and quaint, fanciful facts.

Or were they? Without doubt the story about him and the Queen of Elfland has given me many a moment for ponderous thought and reflection. Thomas regularly visited neighbouring estates for hunting trips and that included one near Melrose Abbey which, as the crow flies, is only a few miles away. How can I discount the idea of him catching a snooze under the Eildon tree, by the waterfall at Bogle Burn, and being kissed by a beautiful woman from a place betwixt and between? How can I ridicule the possibility of seven years in a land of elves? After all, I am a stone with thoughts, observations and feelings stuck up here in a wall of ordinary construction with mortar connecting and securing me to other less magical pieces of rock. Quite simply I am an unexceptional stone with exceptional qualities. It is definitely not my place to dispute the myths and stories so all I can add is that Thomas was a fair landlord and, despite having a bit of a temper, was not known as a liar or a cheat. His prophesies did indeed come true on more occasions than not, and as a man who created inspiring poetic verse his subsequent title of Thomas the Rhymer seems well deserved. My dear old Rab was not in quite the same league!

Still, there are nights when the light seems to catch in a particular way and an orange glow seeps into the landscape giving the dusk a clarity belonging only to itself. In those fragments of time the realms of another world seem infinitely possible and I wonder whether the rustling grass holds an elf or two, gathering snippets of gleaming gossip, before returning with reports to Thomas and his Queen. Whether it is just my imagination searching for inspiration I wish Thomas well wherever he may be, and perhaps the thought of him enjoying eternity shrouded in romantic myth and legend is one that leads others to hope for a similar fate. Brrrrrrr! A chill just blew across me.

The days are definitely becoming shorter so autumn must be fast approaching, and soon, those moments of romance in the sunshine, of love and whispered nothings, will be replaced by evenings on comfy sofas pulled close to a roaring fire. Now, let me tell you that of all the sentiments, fates and feelings love has to be the one that is all pervading and persuasive. While I do not mean to eavesdrop there is little I can do when people share their most intimate secrets a few feet away from my permanent spot in this world. I have listened to so many protestations of love over the years ... you would think that nothing else mattered. And while I try to empathise with those who hold such deep emotion for another being or entity it does stretch my sentimental core to the absolute limit! Not being able to speak adds to my frustration as, having witnessed the beginning ... the middle ... the end of many an affair with all its passion and ardour, I could share a few words of wisdom. Still, it has kept me entertained, and not a little amused, over the years. Just last Sunday a couple sat in the sunshine after a lunch of roast pork and raspberry cheesecake and shared, with many a fond kiss, the happy memories of their time together. May they have many more ... for aw' that.

Without wanting to seem ungrateful for the various visitors that come to see me, and the tinkling waters of a well stocked fish pond, the placement of this small restaurant does cause me some reason to moan and grumble. Quite simply I am hidden. After all, I can hardly jump up and down to be noticed by a wider public! On more than one occasion I have wanted to share a few words of objection as this tiny hamlet has evolved into the extensive village it is today. Life was pleasantly pastoral for a long time until somebody invented the industrial revolution! What a noisy, dirty time that was and almost disastrous for me when people started pinching the stones from my tower to build a local mill. While it might have changed the fortunes of a few such industry disappeared long ago as did the railway that used to plough through the landscape with trains blowing steam, and raucous whistles, to herald their arrival or departure. Not that I needed

Rhymers Tower

these additional signals as my foundations were aware of any train progressing up or down the line long before anybody waiting patiently on the platform. The tingling sensation created by these huge lumps of iron rumbling over the tracks was quite novel really, and rather different to that produced by the now endless stream of road traffic and mixed assortment of vehicles regularly arriving at my garage for essential fuel, a local paper or packet of cheese and onion crisps.

Not that many of those drivers come and pay me the courtesy of a visit. No, they are too busy trying to carve out their own place in history to worry about me and mine. Yet it would be pertinent for them to remember that we are all born of the earth to whence we will return though, without wanting to sound superior, my life span is far greater than theirs. Little visitors arrive from the local school with more awareness but the young have a pure simplicity of judgement that is often lost with the busy pressures of age and time. They come with their teachers and drawing books to acknowledge my historical significance giggling, shouting and glad to be free from the confines of stuffy classrooms. Aware that they might be drawing me I feel strangely proud and try to look happy, benign even, for my portrait though there is very little to be done about my permanently static grin. This then reminds me that while I might wish for more, being happy with that given and allowed, is a lesson we must all learn. As I notice the blond hair, brown eyes or strong bones of my excited observers it makes me wonder whether there are any descendants of Thomas Learmont amongst them. Connections have certainly been made in the past ... all the way to Russia and the poet, Mikhail Lermontov who claimed to be a son, of a son, of a son!

Beneath a heaven of storms his poetry made him famous so sweet old Rab was not in his league either! Still without my whispered words I would not have been given existence and even though my future may lie in the hands of others past debts must also be acknowledged. Life has been interesting, varied and even colourful so while older and a little more weathered my days seem set to continue. After all, both the garage and restaurant came and sat on my doorstep and then, to add insult to injury, took my name so at the very least a little cherishing is in order especially when I have the benefits of both heritage and beauty. Still pride comes before a fall and that thought is a little too close to home so let us move on to consider that as an unlikely trio we can also provide fuel for your car, food for your mind and a wee bit of fancy for your soul. No wonder I can still be filled with good cheer as another full moon shines bright in the darkened sky and a deer moves with quiet stealth beneath the rapidly growing leylandi trees. In ancient folk lore deer are meant to be fairies in disguise so perhaps this one is searching for a few elves to join in some fun and frivolity while the rest of the world sleeps and dreams of escape to places where anything is possible ... where even stones can have stories to share.

Rhymers Tower wall detail

Poetry

The Coal Bearers of Kitleyknowe, Harlawmuir and Macbiehill

By Anita John

It's raining, pouring
from the sky, like stones,
and bouncing, bursting
from the ground, like me.
Me reeling. Barefoot.
Tramping and splashing
and shouting. Breaking
the surface with cries.

We children. Laughing,
with the rain. Washing
us clean, running in rivers
down our skin, through
our clothes, the dirt
flooding from us.

And daylight.
Us playing.
In white light.
Bright April rags.

We're to stop now.
I'm to pick up
my creel and crawl.
We're wet, but we'll
wrought a fine sweat.
Down here, in the
vaults, in the void.
Still reeling,

we fumble
this tunnel
of coal light,
crawl blinkered

and blank
into shade.

We're weighted,
broken and saddled
like donkeys, we stumble
this seam without space.

I'm youngest.
A navvie, who'll marry
a boy in grimed grace.
And carry, from shaft
head to daylight,
his children, 'til the
black sightless face
strikes me dumb.

Historical Note: Coal mining is one of the oldest industries of this part of Peeblesshire and children were used to work in the mines during the 18th and early 19th centuries. Boys and girls as young as six years old would bear the coal to the surface, carrying creels, and working for 12 to 14 hours each day without resting (from three in the morning until four or five in the evening). Sixteen-year old girls were known to carry up to 100 kg (2 cwt) per journey. Until 1799 colliers and their wives, sons and daughters were effectively serfs, attached to the soil and passed with the land on any change of proprietor. In 1911 the employment of women and children in mines was finally abolished.

Land previously mined at Kitleyknowe, looking across to Harlawmuir, now reinstated farmland.

The Kirk o' The Forest
By Rosalie Saunders

February is a magical time to visit the ruins of Dryburgh Abbey when the snowdrops carpet the icy earth. But come in May, to the Kirk Wynd, just up from the Market Place in Selkirk, when the pink prunus blossoms dance in the Spring sunshine, inviting you to explore the remains of the Kirk o' The Forest and the graveyard of tumbled stones and newer piles around.

As you pull back the slot of the huge, heavy iron gate, you see just ahead the roofless ruin of the stone-built Kirk o' The Forest. Scottish Kings used to hunt in Ettrick Forest which once covered much of the hills in this Border region. Walk on to where another iron gate has replaced the original wooden door of the church. Above is the bell which is still tolled for a funeral. Occasionally it is heard, when a reveller, a bit worse for the wear, decides to give it laldy in the wee sma''oors! There is a story, written as a poem, when instead of a metal chain attachment to the bell, there was a rope. Through time, it frayed and broke. The Town Council of the day met to decide how it could be repaired. Eventually, a sailor who had been jailed for being disorderly, mended it for one shilling, but the bill for the Town Council's deliberations in the Cross Keys came to twelve shillings!

The Christian needs of Selkirk were first met by the monks of the Benedictine Order of Tyron in France, who occupied a wooden Abbey at Lindean. St. Mary and St. John the Evangelist, was founded in 1113, by Earl David who became King David 1 of Scotland. He and his wife Queen Margaret did much to further Christianity and education in Scotland. Even today David is still a popular boy's name. In 1125 this Abbey moved to become a stone structure in the more fertile lands of Kelso. The original Kirk o' the Forest was established on this site around the 12th Century and was of Catholic organization. The same building was used come the Reformation until burned down in 1534 by George Hoppringle of Torwoodlee.

The Kirk o' the Forest or Kirk of Selkirk is mentioned in old Border Records. A large plaque beside the kirk door declares that William Wallace was proclaimed Guardian of Scotland on this site in 1298,

The Kirk o' The Forest

in the name of Lord John, King John Balliol. The kirk stood not far from the Castle or Peel of Selkirk, which was a wooden structure built both by Scots and English at various times over the years. In 1302 there was a garrison of 73 billeted there. Unfortunately there are no remains left or proper excavation done.

Going into the present ruin of the protestant structure built in 1747, and used as the Parish Kirk till 1861, you are struck by the light and airiness of the interior. Athough there were allocated galleries of seating to guilds like the Merchants & Shoemakers, or Gentry like the Kers of Roxburgh, there is but one central aisle. Nowadays, very early on Easter morning, an ecumenical service is held there, the voices joining with the dawn birdsong, or like last year with the accompaniment of an enormous crow perched on top of the bell. Hopefully now, the Kirk Folk are less judgemental and self righteous, fingering out sinners and witches, and are working together on such projects as Fresh Start Borders supplying household goods for the local homeless.

Along the walls are stones inscribed with the names of the departed. Very interesting is the alcove of the 'Murray Aisle'. The name dates back to when it was de Moravia in 1280, with lands at Falahill, and Philiphaugh. The female spouse isn't named, unless she has a famous father. John Murray, the Outlaw's wife was Lady Margaret Hepburn, daughter of Patrick, Earl of Bothwell, 1519 and John Murray, MP's wife, Eleanor Hamilton, granddaughter of the Duke of Hamilton 1759. The notice at the entrance alludes to the Maternal forebears of Franklin D. Roosevelt, 32nd President of the United States, being buried there. Further along the wall are tombstones of the 20th century, that of William Connochie 1906 and his son, 1928 both MRCVS; George Roberts, the Provost 1910, Craig Brown, Historian; J.B. Selkirk, Poet, and John Lang, a Sheriff of Selkirk.

Coming out of the Kirk turn right past a memorial to the Father in Law of Mungo Park, the explorer of the Niger: 'Thomas Anderson, Surgeon,1850, erected by the working class of the County and town of Selkirk as testimony to the esteem he earned among them during a laborious practice of 43 years. In remembrance his name is revered and his death lamented as that of a friend.' Is there a Medical Man or Woman to whom this would apply now with so many part-timers and NHS24 ? The stone path leads on to grass, cut by the Council and the clippings left to rot on the surface.

Many of the headstones are unreadable and some lie tumbled one on the other. Some of the heavy slabs and iron railings put up to thwart the body snatching of Burke and Hare in the 1800s lie crumbling and twisted. New black & gold stones with bright coloured flowers in front now occupy the land where the cholera victims of 1847 were laid to rest.

Sit on one of the seats looking towards Philiphaugh where Leslie defeated Montrose and slaughtered the camp followers. Beyond is the quiet beauty of the Linglie hills and valleys of Ettrick and Yarrow. Breathe in the fresh clean air. The Haining Estate endowed to the town by Andrew Nimmo Smith is on your left. Some remember the Pageant held there and the Royal Company of the Queens Bodyguard of Archers shooting for the Selkirk Silver Arrow, entertained afterwards with a Riddle of Claret. Others walking their dogs round the Loch look out for the Grey Lady Ghost. The names of Selkirk are all around, Muir, and Stewart, Drapers, Clapperton/ Mitchell Photographer, Tom Scott the Artist; the obelisk of the Good Templars, Soldier, Shoemaker, Royal Burgh Standard Bearer...

The words on a more recent headstone make you smile. Ross Brownlee was a well kent face, a Weaver and a Walker with strong ideas on diet and use of mothballs. Akin to Spike Milligan's. ' I said I was ill,' the inscription is 'Nae preservatives and I still deid'. Drilled through the stone are holes as if the moths had the last word!

Even when the clouds hang like clumps of dirty washing and the rain slashes horizontal at your face, there is an attractiveness at walking through the Kirkyaird. The auld names live through the ruins . It's as if they whisper in the wind. 'We weren't aye right, but we've done our bit. Now you carry on to make this world a better place.'

Voices of Ghosts
By Claire Bowles

'Why? Why me?
Why now?
I hate you. Do you know that?
I HATE you!'

Marie gave up trying to turn the engine over and snapped off her seatbelt. She let the belt retract freely, knowing from experience that the metal clip would fly back and smash into the driver's side window with a force that would nearly chip and shatter toughened glass. She jumped, then smiled with vindictive pleasure, as the sharp crack echoed in the tight, enclosed space. Serve you right, you little sod, she thought.

Getting out, she wrapped her coat more snugly around her, trying to close off the gaps that were allowing the chilly October wind to penetrate all three layer of clothing. The little silver zip hung uselessly, jostling against the rush of air. Whenever anybody asked – which thankfully wasn't often – she told them it was broken, a chink in the track; but the truth was she could no longer fasten it over the bulge around her middle that refused to go away no matter how many diet companies she paid.

Marie took the three steps necessary to cross to the front of her little silver Corsa, and grasped the bonnet. She had to position her hands carefully, making sure to avoid the sharp edges where the once sleek lines had rusted away, and the flaking sections which were soon to follow suit. Taking one deep breath, she heaved, revealing the innards of the car. Then she peered downwards, lips pursed, eyes scanning black unidentified bit to black unidentified bit. She had no idea what she was looking for. No idea what any of these things did. It was just what one did when one's piece of junk car stopped working abruptly at the crest of a hill in the middle of nowhere.

Cars whipped past at an alarming speed. There was no hard shoulder as such, but the tarmac was wider here, providing enough space for the car to come wheezing to a halt, just about out of harm's way. Marie looked optimistically at the vehicles as they passed. Maybe some helpful man would stop, come jogging over and rescue her from the calamity that was her life. Doubtful. Maybe ten years ago. Maybe not even then.

Sighing, she slammed the bonnet back down, watching another few metal flakes drift downwards. The scraping crunch of the clasp connecting rent through the air at the same time that the first droplet hit the roof of the silver Corsa with a dainty plink. Marie missed it, staring off into nothingness, cursing her luck. Frustration bubbling over, she aimed a kick at the dirt spattered bumper, then grinned evilly, before exhaling in a sigh. The damn boot would probably refuse to open for six months now. It was temperamental.

Now what? Her B&B was in Peebles, surely not far away. She could probably leave the car here and walk; no-one would touch it. Good luck to them if they got it going. She shifted from foot to foot, undecided. She was wearing heels, something she rarely did, and it might be four hundred yards, or four miles. Then another drop fell, swiftly followed by several more. They bounced off the Corsa, falling with enough force to rebound and explode in the air. Forget that idea then. She turned around, looking back at the big hotel she had just passed. A Macdonald's. She'd seen it on the internet when she'd searched for places to stay, but it was easily out of her budget. She could see why, eyes picking out the immaculate greens and oyster shell bunkers of the golf course. She could phone the RAC from there.

Marie took one step, then hesitated. The car park was bursting with Landrovers and Jaguars and chic sports cars that she couldn't name. Inside would be full of beautifully manicured wives and high-flying business types. She'd stick out like a sore thumb. A poor sore thumb.

She drummed her fingers on the bonnet as she deliberated, the sound hiding the increased tempo of the rain. Then the deluge started. The heavens opened and deposited wave after wave of moisture. It was the type of rain that drenched you in thirty seconds, less if you were wearing a cheap cagoule which had long ago given up any claim to be waterproof. Someone up there is laughing at me, Marie thought. It would have to be the hotel, then. She took one, last sweeping glance across the landscape, searching for another option. Trees, fields, hills, a river, an old ruin. Nothing.

'Dam-mit!' She drew out the word, still reluctant, but the rain was unrelenting.

Marie took two steps, pausing to turn her face away as a truck zoomed past, spraying her with muck and water, the back draft collecting up her hair and mussing it into a tangled mess.

'Oh come on!' she shouted.

She shook her head, tears of exasperation forming in her eyes. Then her gaze fell again on the ruin. It was a pitiful sight: roof gone, walls half-collapsed, standing lonely at the top of an unimpressive hill. The rain swirled around it like mist. It looked forlorn, abandoned. A bit like her. Without having consciously made the decision, she found herself turning her back on the dry and warmth of the hotel, eyes fixed on the broken castle remains. She came to her senses a little when faced with the waist-height barbed wire fence, but somehow she'd already made up her mind. She struggled over, inelegant and ungainly, then plunged forward into the wet grass, heels sinking into the mud.

The closer she got, the more it revealed itself. And it was not a pretty sight. Lichen was devouring the outer walls, which were crumbling at the corners. The ground surrounding the place was littered with stones that had already fallen. The arrow slit window had worn away so that the average-sized person could probably squeeze through the hole. Here the top of the wall had dipped. Marie had the feeling that if the window ever extended to reach the top of the wall, that whole side of the place would soon topple, disappearing into the hill over time.

Marie circled the ruin. It wasn't big, maybe ten metres by nine metres. One wall, the back wall from her initial viewpoint on the road, was completely gone, the stone eroded away to ground level. It was like an invitation. She stepped inside, catching sight of her little broken Corsa through the slit window. It was a bizarre sight. Closeted by the ancient walls, she felt like she was in another world. The car did not belong.

She shivered, half from the cold and wet, half from a sense of wonder.

'What am I doing here?' she wondered aloud.

'Sheltering from the rain?'

The voice came from behind her, and Marie whirled, one hand grasping her chest above her heart, trying to still the frantic pounding while her head decided whether it was going to scream.

'Oh!' she said, finding the owner of the words.

'Sorry, did I startle you? I assumed you knew I was here.'

An old man was sitting on a large clump of fallen wall, the individual stone bricks still held together by the tough lime mortar. He was smiling at her benignly, his face protected from the downpour by a grey bunnet, droplets from the saturated cap falling onto a dark green wax jacket. Marie's replying smile faltered on her face as she realised there was something slightly off about his posture. Both hands were hidden behind his back. What was he doing? Was he hiding something?

The old man seemed to notice her suspicion. He brought his arms back around, folding both hands on his knees in a neat steeple.

'Not the best day for sightseeing,' he commented, trying to smooth over the awkward moment.

'No,' Marie agreed with a breathy chuckle. 'It wasn't planned, though. My car's broken down.'

She pointed towards the road behind her, then wished she hadn't. She didn't want him to know she was stuck here. There was something off about him. It was his eyes, maybe. They seemed... not all there.

'There's a hotel down there,' he nodded down the hill towards the Macdonald's. 'I dare say you could phone for someone.'

'Yes. Yes, I was just going to do that.'

'Just thought you'd have a quick look over here first, eh?' he asked.

'Something like that,' Marie agreed.

He must have thought she was mad, traipsing over here in the pouring rain when what she needed was in the opposite direction.

'I like it here, too,' he continued, a knowing look in his eyes. 'The place sort of calls to you, you know?'

'Mmm,' Marie mumbled, non-committal.

'Do you know anything about the ruin?' He paused, so she shook her head. 'Horsburgh Castle, it's called. It was built in the sixteenth century. Nothing impressive to look at now, but it would have been four stories high in its prime. Impressive structure then, or at least that was the idea. Let everybody know how big and strong and rich you were.'

'Huh,' Marie said, realising the old man was waiting for some sort of response. She looked at the tattered remains of the walls that still stood. It was hard to imagine it as he described, strong and powerful.

'My wife used to love it here. She used to say you could feel the history, hear the whisper on the wind of all the folk who had lived and died here all that time ago. Maisie was her name,' he added, tailing off.

'I'm sorry,' Marie said. It was obvious in the way he spoke that she was no longer living. She felt sorry for him; he looked sunken and defeated now, slumping over in sadness, but he was creeping her out with all this talk of ghosts.

She shivered again. The rain was still falling hard, and though the walls provided some protection, shielding her from the wind, she was soaked through and frozen. She ran one hand through her matted curls, pushing them back off her face.

'Well,' she said, trying to sound bright. 'I'm just going to head to the hotel. Make that call.'

The old man ignored her, staring at the ground at his feet. Marie backed away, for some reason unwilling to turn her back on him until she'd put some distance between them.

'Sometimes I think I hear Maisie when I'm here,' he muttered, almost too low for her to hear.

His face grew more morose; it was painful to look at. Marie watched as he reached behind him again, fingers searching for something.

That was enough for her. She turned and scurried out of the ruin, trotting down the hill and across the golf course. She was a sight, wet through and coated in mud. Rather than wait for the RAC, she phoned a taxi to take her to the B&B, then lingered outside, away from the disapproving eyes of the hotel guests.

The B&B was nice. Bright, cheerful, and in the centre of town. A good base to explore from. After a bath and a comfortable sleep, she was looking forward to checking out the sights. She'd worry about the car tomorrow: it wasn't going anywhere. The breakfast smelled good, too, she decided, as she descended the stairs into the little eating area.

There were some local tourist leaflets laid out on the table. One stood out from the others. Picking it up, Marie stared at the picture on the front. Horsburgh Castle. She shuddered again, leftover unease.

'You don't want to go there today,' the B&B owner commented as she filled up her coffee. Marie opened her mouth to correct her, but the woman wasn't done. 'Someone died up there yesterday. An old man, some widower. Killed himself.'

She bustled off, leaving Marie astounded, mouth still open as her eyes filled with tears.

Ruins Triptych
By Dorothy Alexander

Nancy

div ee mind ae thon fellae that bid at the fit ae Queen Street big
fellae wi rid curly hair kinnae English spoken aye hud a golden
retriever mairried on Carrie Johnstone's sister what's her name
again Nancy her that run away frae hame when she wis only
sixteen mind she run away wi that butcher frae Selkirk ae hud a
funny name oh what wis it I cannae juist mind ae wis mairried tae
wi twae wee bairns nice wee things they were they bid next door
tae Hugh's mother an fither aes wife wis a bonny lassie Hugh's
mother helped oot by lookin efter the bairns whiles tae let her oot
tae work for she hud tae sort awthin oot hud tae lairn the business
at least enough tae let her run the shop she worked hard the lassie
kept the business gaun in fact she still runs it yet ee'l huv seen her
if ee've ever been in Wright's the butcher that yin at the corner ae
Tait's Wynd aye winnin prizes fur their pies an their haggis Wright
wis her ain name onywey Nancy an the butcher didnae lest long
she wis back hame or long wi her tail atween her legs mind it
wisnae funny he'd sterted hittin her so they said nae sma wonder
that aes wife wid never huv him back ae got a job wi a butcher in
Peebles drivin their van ae went roond the toon and up the country
sellin meat an eggs an thae kinnae things ah mind ae cowped it
yeah day on the bad bend at Horsbrugh Castle thonder but the
Japs got him in the end he ended up on the Burma railway typhoid
they reckoned an puir Nancy naebody wid look at her so when the
war stertit she joined the Wrens that's how she met that fellae he
wis in the Navy the pair ae them got mairried an came back here
efter the war they hud juist the yin lassie Christine her name wis
awfy clever lassie went tae be a teacher onywey he came up on the
pools on Seturday Bert Shillinglaw wis tellin aes yesterday twae
thoosand aes won no bad eh plenty I could dae wi twae thoosand

Ruins Triptych
By Dorothy Alexander

Red head

ma youngest sister wis right bonny no that I wis ugly or even plain
I hud ma mother's colourin auburn but I hud ower mony freckles
for ma ain likin an kinnae wiry hair ma sister took efter ma fither
blonde curly hair and sic bonny blue een she wis juist a wee doll
when she wis wee grew up tall an slender juist like him aw the
fellaes were efter her it can be a bit ae a curse bein that bonny
ee see a lot ae weemin that're guid lookin thinkin too much ae
theirsels an never bein content or mairryin somebody that's got
plenty money an they're no happy I mind this wummin that lived
in the posh hooses up by the Cross Kirk oo would see her often
when oo wis bairns red-heided she wis a right looker her man
hud plenty money he wis a guid bit aulder than her the story wis
that he'd chased her for years wore her doon eventually gied her
onythin she wantit ee wid see them gaun aboot airm in airm he
wis aye right protective wi her right gentlemanly but tae me there
wis aye a kinnae deid look in her een ma sister wisnae like that she
wis never vain for aw she wis a stunner she wis right freendly an
liked a laugh that juist made the fellaes worse of course they wid
be fawin ower each other tryin tae get a date she wid juist laugh at
them tell them she wisnae ready fur that kinnae thing the man she
ended up wi wis the last yin ee wid ever huv expectit he wis a wee
quiet fellae wid never huv kent he wis there but he hud the awfiest
crush on her she worked in the Store office up the stairs frae the
furnishin he hud tae keep gaun up tae the office tae sort oot orders
an yin day he juist plucked up enough courage tae ask her oot an
he must've nearly fell doon when she said that she wid an that wis
it they were made for each other frae that day on ee never saw him
but he had a smile on aes face it fair did yer hert guid juist tae see
them thegither

Ruins Triptych
By Dorothy Alexander

Wee Audrey's mother

I liked men I'll no deny it although I only ever married yin an that
wis when I wis young an daft I sin got shot ae him he wis a waster
Christina wis his then I hud Shirley her fither wis an insurance
man an then a guid bit later I hud wee Audrey course I hud a bit
ae a reputation when ee live in a wee pliss that's juist natural but
naebody really bothered aes they widnae huv dared I aye worked
I kept ma bairns clean an I wisnae a hame wrecker I nivver took
onybody's man off them there wis only yince I let masel get hurt I
wid've been in ma late twenties by then an he wisnae frae the toon
he came tae be the new manager ae the mill but through the week
he stopped at the hotel I wis workin in till he could find a hoose I
suppose he hud the gift ae the gab an aye seemed tae huv plenty
cash he took aes away yince three days oo hud in a guest hoose in
Kendal I left the bairns wi ma sister he wis gaun tae leave aes wife
an oo were gaun tae move tae Huddersfield but he couldnae dae
it in the end she wis kinnae nervy an he didnae huv it in him tae
leave her I nivver went near a man for a guid while efter that then I
got a job in the chemist the yin that yased tae be on the corner
opposite the Abbey Mr. Sykes whae owned it wis a lovely man a
wee bit aulder but awfy nice an when aes wife died I wis aes
comfort he wis right guid tae me I wanted fur nuthin he wid've
mairried aes but I tellt him I wis quite happy the wey I wis I liked
ma independence an I think there wis a bit ae him that wis gled
aboot that really for he liked aes peace an quiet wee Audrey wis his

Cross Kirk, Peebles

The Clintz Rotunda
By John Milligan

By ony road The Clintz is up a hill
It's fermin jist that nearer tae the sky
Auld farrant days it hid a threshin mill
But noo it's a tae sheep wi pens in-bye

Yet still that pennage fences aff a ring
A wa o stanes fornent whit wis the barn
A mind it as a bonnie ferlie thing
But roofless noo an wa'heids maistly fa'en

An engine hoose fur horse tae walk aroon
Tae turn the gears tae thresh or heist or crush
The flair tae be the maist befittin groon
The wa's wi gaps fur swappin sough fur sough

The orange dome wis seen frae mony airts
The cleekit pantiles neebors every yin
Were washit clean by a the bluisterin blasts
Were bleachit bricht an moss-free fae the sun

Yet corn lang gane an gearins used nae mair
The wa's wis stappit up tae mak a bield
But itchin beasts maun scart the mortar sair
A puckle o the stanes began tae yield

Then in the Seventies cam an awfie gale
That raxed at a the rafters yont their pooer
An doon the tiles an timmers fell an skailed
The toorie a awa tae bits an stoor

The ruin's near on thirty fit across
But ne'er an inch o horse-walk tae be seen
Taen ower by a muckle elder bush
That ettles tae reprise the dome in green

At the Ruins, We Sharpen Our Spears
By Chris Bowles

It escapes me. The cold winter. The frost. Her eyelids fluttering as we passed her into the fire. No, I can't remember it now that summer is here. The trees nuzzling the wide river; blending into deep green waves in the breeze. The flashing grey underside of a buzzard's wings. The mound of stones on the hill beside me, hot to the touch. I sharpen my spear.

We came to this place often, her and I, when we were young. The Ruins on the mountain. The place where we can speak to ghosts. My father is here, as is hers. Their ashes blow up on the wind from the cairns and collect in the tall Songless Stones to swirl and dance like grey butterflies in the moonlight. All our ancestors do this. She is doing this now.

We would come here in summers like this and bring stones from the river as gifts. We placed them on the cairns where our fathers sleep and then lay back on the stones feeling the warmth through our clothes. We would stare up at the clouds rolling by. We would kiss, nothing more

But as I sharpen my spear, I struggle to recall our times here. They are distant and as though fog on the hills on cold mornings. But I know we came because it is a holy place. To kiss at the Ruins, to watch the clouds, to sharpen a spear makes these things blessed and full of life.

A sacred place. Each year, when harvests grow ripe, all the people climb the mountain to the Ruins. They leave their stones and speak with the dead as the priests go to the Songless Stones and incant to the gods and all our ancestors. And during this time, our warriors bring the gift to the altar. We all spit on this gift as it's led to the stone in the centre. The Chief Priest pushes its head to the stone, makes it bow. And then he makes it pray. Not the prayers it would have used in its own village. No; our prayers, our words. It cries and thrashes and no longer looks human; is no longer human, not since our warriors captured it in the field of battle. The Chief Priest lifts his robes to reveal his two daggers, of flesh and bronze. We scream and hum. The bronze dagger is lifted and then tastes the sacrifice's blood on the altar. The gift is brought to the pyre and set alight.

Above this, hunted boars roast and soak in its essence and strength. We will feast on it. And sing. And dance. In this way, the gift will be given to all the people and help us thrive in the cold months . The ashes from the pyre will go to the fields.

We married on a night like this; when the boar was shared and the pyre was little more than cinder. We stood with other couples in front of the Chief Priest, naked and shivering. Though we'd known each other all our lives, this was a moment to relish and fear. And as the fire died, we lay with each other among the cairns and emerged a single being. She gave me this wet stone that now rides the blade of my spear.

We lived a content life; I the warrior, her the gardener. And our son now carries a spear in the war band. But our life is no more, and in her absence I forget many things. My spear is sharper now, and can cut the memories from this world.

Memories of how she is lost to me, of how the yearly battle has become war tide.

The Old Ones know the beginnings of this world. How the sea once dried and men walked into this land. How the gods led them to the stones and metals of the earth and taught them how to shape these and give them a soul. My own spear was made by a man in the mountains many years ago who turned rock into rivers of metal that filled a void in a mould, much as she flowed through my existence. Her ghost from the Ruins is now a spear that will split the world.

The Gods gave us these things that we might bring life from the earth, and protect that life from others who would take it. Others like the people by the sea.

Since the beginning of the world, we have met them on the field of battle by the wide river. Our warriors and theirs with spears and swords like shafts of burning light. An awesome sight as we face each other on the hills. My son has now seen this, and his heart now beats with our drums. But we do not fight. We have not fought since men can remember. Blood is a precious thing, and not lightly spilt. To die in battle is to watch your crops die and hear your people starve from your place in the Ruins. Instead, we survive through the gifts; the battles of the lone champions and the trade of one of our beloved warriors into the hands of the other. These are gifts to the gods, and they have saved many a generation of our people from destruction.

Each year has been the same. Our warriors see their warriors. We line the ridges with our golden spears and hurl curses at their gods, their mothers and their wives. Our champions meet and fight until the first falls. I have been a champion for ten summers now. Ten men have tasted my sword and notched my shield. The Old Ones say I am the best they have ever seen.

But the last fight, I do not remember. I do not remember their king's son facing me. A boy the age of my son. I do not remember him shaking, the dishevelled blonde hair, or the red rings around his eyes. He shook, but still he faced me. He wore the clothes of a God. He wore over his shoulders a silvery stranded cloak from an incomprehensible land, a circlet of gold hung from his neck, a sword belt with jewels as big as my eyes from his hips, he held a shimmering bronze dagger patterned with sun spots and the swirling patterns of the stars. His father, the king stood behind him among the warriors on the hill. Pride and fear were in his eyes, but confidence all the same.

I close my eyes now to hold back the memory. He lunged. I moved away. He lunged again. I backhanded his arm and his dagger dropped. He fell. I removed his life from the world.

His father stood still for a moment. His long grey beard waving like a stormy cloud. His hand went to his sword. There was a sound like the clatter of wild horses on the earth as the warriors of his tribe lifted their spears and held them ready for war. Behind me, where the sun sat idle, the shadows of our warriors and their raised spears looked like a black boar; its spiny mane raised and poised for the strike. The ritual had come too far for the exchange of gifts. The blood of our warriors would be spilled and I would likely never see my family again.

But then our king walked to me, deep sadness in his eyes.

'My friend,' he said to me 'it should never have come to this.'

He turned to the warriors and pointed to his own son, the prince, who he loved dearly. The boy came forward, suddenly unsure of what he was to do. The king would not look at him. He instead raised his arms in the sign of the gift to their ruler, and he walked away. I heard him moan as he went.

I looked at the prince, and he looked at me. His face hardened as realization settled on him. His eyes pleaded, his breath came quick. I do not remember the fear he showed. I cannot recall his pleas as two of their warriors accepted the gift and led him away.

I looked back to the hill opposite. Their king's eyes had never left me. They were solid things, grey like the new metals that are being made in the hills. His hand still held the hilt of his sword, his knuckles red and white, but soon he turned and walked back to the sea. His warriors followed, but slowly and with many a backwards glance at the field. I knew then that battle had been averted, but not war. For the first time we did not have a gift for the pyre.

We returned along the river road to our people. The Old Ones cried and pulled at their hair when we failed to return with the gift of trade. They ran up to the mountain to the Ruins and we could hear them all that night praying in the Songless Stones.

She and I, and our son, made prayers as well. And I prayed more than I ever had that the soul of their prince would not haunt our family. We did this for many nights. And then the night came that I dare not remember. The night when the sea people flooded our village like a fat hungry river. They kicked at our doors and grabbed at our hair. They torched the roofs of our houses and slaughtered our cattle in the pens. And then, the horror. We were bound and led to the Ruins. All the people. We entered the Songless Stones where their king stood atop the altar and cast a smile on us all. The vile king looked at my family and pointed to my wife. Their warriors grabbed her and brought her to the altar. The king leapt from the stone and made her bow. My son and I tried to run forward. We screamed and shook and railed at the king with every curse we knew. But their warriors held us. And we watched as their king took the soul of our family from us.

But I cannot remember this. I must not remember this.

We sharpen our spears this summer. Each stroke whistles its tune and rends the air clean of the past. I live now for my wet stone. This stone that came to me from the river and gives my spear its terrible voice. This stone, delivered from her hands to mine many years ago when we were wed; though I have no memory of this.

Our horses will ride the hills this summer; from the Ruins to the wide river, from the Songless Stones to the plains of the sea where their boats creak and clack. We ride our hungry war-hogs bristling their spiny furs to the old man in the sun.

We seek a gift.

Note - The inspiration for this story came from the cairns and stone circles at Whitton Edge, near Hownam.

Nicholas
By Jo Dubé

I am confused by this thing they call Time. I remember so many things, and they all seem to be past; but how can I be sure?

Humans are slow when they begin their journey through time. Gradually, they get faster and faster, and then they begin to slow down again. My human memories run one after the other in sequence, but I cannot reliably tell whether they really came before everything else, or whether they are yet to come.

When I was human, I had a name. I remember when I was slow, on all fours, hearing my mother call my name. My mother's voice told me that I was safe, and so long as I retain that memory, I know that I will still be safe.

I was human: so what am I now? Am I alive because so many believe in me still? I died in the Year of Our Lord 343, and from then until now (but what is Now?), they have told stories about me.

I seem to recall a time when the church here was ruined. It was a place for cats to climb and bats to roost; beloved by the people who live around and nearby, and used from time to time by them for worship; but open to the winds and rain, roofless, not covered. Is this Now? Is it really later than Then, when I was young?

Johanna opened the door to me. I noticed the tear stains on her cheeks, but when she put her finger on her lips I didn't say anything. Sara was stirring something.

'That smells good!' I exclaimed. She turned and smiled a greeting at me, and I was shocked by how pale she was.

'Nonna! Enna!' she called. 'Nicholas is here, and he wants chicken mash for dinner.' I laughed jovially, but it rang hollow. Enna came in to finish setting the table. Nonna followed slowly. Her head was bowed, and she didn't look at me at all.

Martin came in as Sara began to serve the meal. He stopped short when he saw me.

'Of course, it's Wednesday, isn't it?' he said flatly. 'Welcome, Nicholas. It's good to see you, lad.' But his tone belied his words.

I glanced at Sara: her lips were folded and her face was stony. Nonna was looking at her plate, and Enna was twisting her handkerchief. Johanna looked back at me: her eyes were bright, and she shook her head very slightly.

I made myself eat heartily. I saw Johanna swallowing hard, as if her food was full of stones. None of the others managed to eat even as little as she did, and no-one spoke.

Eventually, Martin pushed his chair back and went out to attend to the stock, without a word. Sara began to clear the table. I decided to leave them in peace, but I was arrested by a tiny sob from Nonna. I held out my arms and all three girls came and crowded round me.

'Won't you tell me what it is?' I pleaded. Sara shook her head. Nonna buried her face in my shoulder and sobbed. Enna gripped my other shoulder so hard that I felt her nails.

'Why? said Sara harshly. 'Nothing and no-one can help us now!' She sat down hard on the nearest chair and sobbed.

I looked down, straight into Johanna's eyes.

'I'll tell you,' she said. Nonna wailed in protest, but Johanna just raised her voice. 'It can't do any harm. It can't make things worse, anyway.'

'Of course it can make things worse, idiot!' snapped Enna. 'If Nicholas tells anyone...'

'Nicholas never gossips!' cried Nonna breathlessly. This about-turn stunned everyone into silence for a moment.

'That is true,' said Sara at last. 'Very well, Johanna. But none of you – not even Nicholas – are to breathe a word of this to Martin.' I promised to keep their counsel.

'It's very simple, really,' said Johanna. 'Father's most recent investments were unsuccessful. He found out today that he has lost money instead of making it. And our neighbour's eldest son called today with his father to ask permission to court Nonna.'

'But I don't see –' I said foolishly. Then I closed my eyes. 'There is no money to pay for the dowry,' said a voice I didn't recognise as my own.

'Nicholas, don't walk out,' cried Johanna. I opened my eyes, and realised that the three girls had backed away and I was half way through the door. 'I trusted you. Don't walk out on us!'

'I'm sorry," I said. 'I'm really sorry. Of course you can trust me. I was just thinking.' I turned to Sara. 'Martin will be in from doing the chores in a minute, won't he? Is there any more of that spiced ale?'

My mind was working so hard that I was almost as silent as Martin whilst we shared a drink. Perhaps that reassured him. As I left, he gripped my shoulder for a moment and said gruffly,

'I hope you'll still come and see us, Nicholas, whatever else happens.'

'Of course I will,' I said, and meant it.

Then I walked home slowly, my mind whirling.

What am I? I was human once. I am not human now.

Once upon a time (I remember this) a king named Alexander found an ornate wooden cross here in this place. The cross lay upon a stone which bore my name, *locus sancti Nicolai episcopi*, and when the King's people dug near it they found a burial cist containing bones and ashes.

It was obvious to Alexander and his people that the bones were mine. They did not ask themselves why my bones should be there, so far away from my home. All they knew was that I was a holy man of God, and that meant that this place, associated with my name, must be a holy place for God. Neither am I certain that the bones were not mine. It is true that I was buried in the city that made me a bishop, although I never was an ordained priest. But my bones were moved at least once.

Because of the cross upon a stone that bore my name, and because of the cist, King Alexander built a church and founded a priory here. The order he chose was founded to care for Christian captives. (I was imprisoned for my faith, once upon a time, by an emperor who was both greedy and fearful.) The friars also cared for the community around them, and so they provided the first hospital in the area. They looked after the sick in their own homes, and they fed those who were poor. Theirs was the first school in the vicinity, and they welcomed the local people to their church services.

The church was a simple square building, with the domestic buildings (dormitories and kitchens, the hospital and the library) to the North. It is an almost universal tradition to put the domestic offices to the South of the church, so that they are not in shadow. But King Alexander and the friars did not want to cover the ground where the cist had been interred. They made a shrine for the cross and the stone it lay upon, and it was many years before the pilgrims stopped coming.

Sometimes I wonder what part of me was it that saw these things happening, and what part of me it is that still comes back to this place.

Luckily, it was Spring, and the girls kept their window propped open at night. It was easy for me to creep around the side of the house and wait for all the bedtime sounds to die away. When I was sure everyone was asleep, I reached up and threw a leather purse onto the windowsill.

Nonna's wedding was all the more joyful because it had almost never happened. She was radiant, her sisters were delighted and her parents were proud and somewhat tearful. Johanna danced with me and whispered in my ear,

'I'm sure it was something to do with you, Nicholas! Wasn't it you?'

'Was what me?' I asked. 'Surely one of your father's investments came out well after all.' She laughed, and as the music changed she whirled away to dance with a new partner.

I noticed the doctor's son smiling at Enna, and I wasn't too surprised when, after the wedding was over, she and Johanna started giggling in corners. I started planning again. It was proving to be a cold and wet Autumn, so I wouldn't be able to repeat the window trick.

I had an old red cloak at home: it had been my father's, and I had never grown as tall as he was. I only usually wore it at home, so I knew that Martin and his family wouldn't recognise it, not even Johanna the suspicious. So one day I shrouded myself in it and hid a battered leather purse up the sleeve. I wandered up and down, neither going far from their house nor loitering enough to arouse suspicion. My moment came when Enna opened the door to empty the dustpan. Quick as a flash, I threw the purse from the other side of the street and ran before she could look up.

Sara invited me to Enna's betrothal feast, as an old family friend, and Martin confided in me that they had a mysterious benefactor.

'The money isn't from you, is it, Nicholas?' he asked, frowning.

'It's nothing to do with me,' I answered – truthfully: I had no use for the money and they had. I was only passing it on.

'Only I know you have plenty of money, and you are practically part of the family.'

Cross Kirk, Peebles

'Martin, if I thought you would accept money from me, I would have offered it,' I said. He smiled and clapped me on the back.

'Of course you would,' he said. 'I'm sorry I was suspicious.'

Enna's groom was rich, so her wedding was even more splendid than Nonna's. There was more food than all the guests could have eaten in a week, and the spiced beer and mulled wine flowed like milk and water. I knew Johanna wanted to dance with me again, but I didn't want to cause tongues to wag, so I only danced with Sara.

Johanna was the most beautiful of Martin and Sara's three daughters, and she was the best baker, and she was always full of smiles. I wasn't at all surprised when she found a suitor before the Midwinter festival. Sara looked at me kindly when she told me. Johanna was named after my mother, and she had always been my favourite. I'm not sure that I was able to reassure Sara that I was full of happiness for the family, my head was so full of thoughts. I wasn't sure that I dared repeat the red-cloak trick: Johanna had always been so observant.

At last, I came up with the perfect plan. In the dead of night, when I knew the fire would be out, I climbed up onto the roof and

dropped a purse of gold down the chimney.
It fell into Johanna's stocking, which was hanging up to dry.

I will never understand how Time works. It is so very long since this happened, and yet I am still remembered for filling a young girl's stocking in the middle of Winter.

This quiet place in this small town is where I (what is left of the I that was human once) come to be quiet. In this place, people sit on the sun-warmed grass beneath the walls and pray; they sit on the low, broken walls after dark and talk: and they still gather under the sky to worship.

When the pine trees sway in the wind, sometimes I hear my mother's voice calling, 'Nicholas! Nicholas!' And I know that here I am safe, and I always will be.

Note - The inspiration for this story came from Cross Kirk, Peebles where Alexander 111 found a cross and a cist. It was belived that the relics of St Nicholas had been found, and pilgrims came to Peebles for centuries afterwards.

Stones in the Ettrick

Author Biographies

Dorothy Alexander is a writer and creative writing tutor who lives in Galashiels. For more information please see www.dorothyalexander.co.uk

Claire Bowles lives in Peebles with her husband. She is a teacher of English at a school in South Lanarkshire and writes novels for young adults.

Chris Bowles is an American archaeologist with Scottish Borders Council with a keen interest in all things historical, loves writing and hopes to do much more in the future!

Dorothy Bruce – Previously involved with the restoration of a Victorian pier, and organising an annual walking and arts festival. Since returning to the Borders she is concentrating on writing.

Russell Bruce is Books Editor of For Argyll. He has worked in publishing and advertising and was for 8 years a board member of Loch Lomond and The Trossachs National Park.

Iona Carroll has published short stories in the UK and Australia. At present, she is working on the second novel of her trilogy, 'The Story of Father Vic'.

Gwen Chessell is a graduate and former member of staff of the University of Aberdeen. Her first publications were in the field of medical education but she now writes historical biography.

Julian Colton's poetry publications include Something for the Weekend (Scottish Borders Council, 2001), Two Che Guevaras (Scottish Borders Council, 2007) and Everyman Street (Smokestack Publishing, 2009). He has also published a book of children's ghost stories The Looking Glass Years (Scottish Borders Council, 2004).

In 2008 he was CREATE writing fellow for Dumfries and Galloway Council. He co-edits The Eildon Tree magazine.

Jo Dubé comes from a family of writers, and grew up in rural, bilingual south-west Wales. After a variety of careers, she completed an MSc in Creative Writing at Edinburgh University and is currently working on a novel.

Oliver Eade – (www.olivereade.co.uk): Retired doctor. Publications: 30+ short stories; children's novels, Moon Rabbit and Northwards; teenage fantasy, The Terminus (awaiting publication). Play, The Gap short-listed for Rowan Tree Competition 2009.

Chris Fairgrieve –An ecologist by training, Chris Fairgrieve lives and works in the Scottish Borders. Having published poetry in several anthologies this is an early venture into short story writing.

Vee Freir is a Clinical Psychologist who writes in her spare time. As well as poetry, she has also written a self-help book for stress called START to Stress Less.

Pamela Gordon was chief executive of two English local authorities and held a number of public appointments. She now writes various articles and mainly historical fiction.

Lynne Henderson – After recently completing an honours degree in Literature and Art History with the Open University, Lynne went on the do a two year diploma with the OU in Creative Writing.

Jane Houston Green is a professional actor who has also been writing for a number of years. She has had a play produced and won a short competition.

Campbell Hutcheson – a Glaswegian, experienced 20 years as a print journalist before turning to writing plays and short stories. He is working on a non-fiction book and studying interactive media.

Anita John writes poetry and short fiction and is a creative writing tutor for Edinburgh University's Open Studies department.

She is Convenor of the Pentland Writers Group and lives in the most north-easterly corner of the Scottish Borders. http://www.west-linton.org.uk/content/pentlands-writers-group

Bridget Khursheed is a poet and geek based in the Borders; published widely in magazines including The Rialto, The Eildon Tree and The Shop. Good on mountains, bad on towers.

Robert Leach, a former chair of Borders Writers Forum, was educated at Pembroke College, Cambridge. He is the author of over twenty books, the latest being the epic The Journey to Mount Kailash.

Lis Lee – A former journalist, Lis Lee lives and writes in Kelso. Her work has been published in several Scottish literary magazines and anthologies and her work has appeared in New Writing Scotland

John Milligan – Leased Clintz Cottage 1971, beginning five years sophisticating the whole structure of Edinburgh Festival Fringe. Back to schoolmaster's hours to prioritise political playwriting, songwriting and prizewinning poetry. Now in clover.

Dougie Morrison – born in Glasgow and moved to Galashiels many years ago, and enjoys writing about whatever he sees, hears or experiences in life.

Tom Murray – Published poet and fiction writer. His latest play Tangents appeared at the 2010 Edinburgh International Fringe. Most recently Writer In Residence to Clackmannanshire. Co-edits the Eildon Tree. www.tommurray.org

Carol Norris – Grew up in Nottinghamshire near to that part of Sherwood Forest which remains. Has lived in the Borders since 1984. Recently co-opted as third Editor on The Eildon Tree magazine.

Arthur Parsons lives in Coldstream where he writes poems and plays. He's written and directed an award-winning one act play and has another play in production at the moment.

Rosalie Saunders (Brydon) was born in Selkirk, spent some childhood in Malaya, was a Midwife in India, before retirement a Sister at the Borders General Hospital.

Eileen Thornton writes articles and short stories for magazines. Her novel, The Trojan Project, an action thriller, was published in May 2008.

Stow, the three span collection bridge built in 1655

Arch, Kelso Abbey

The following properties mentioned in this anthology are under the care of Historic Scotland -
Dryburgh Abbey, Jedburgh Abbey, Kelso Abbey, Melrose Abbey, Cross Kirk (Peebles), Dere Street Roman Road (Soutra), Greenknowe Tower

Photograph credits

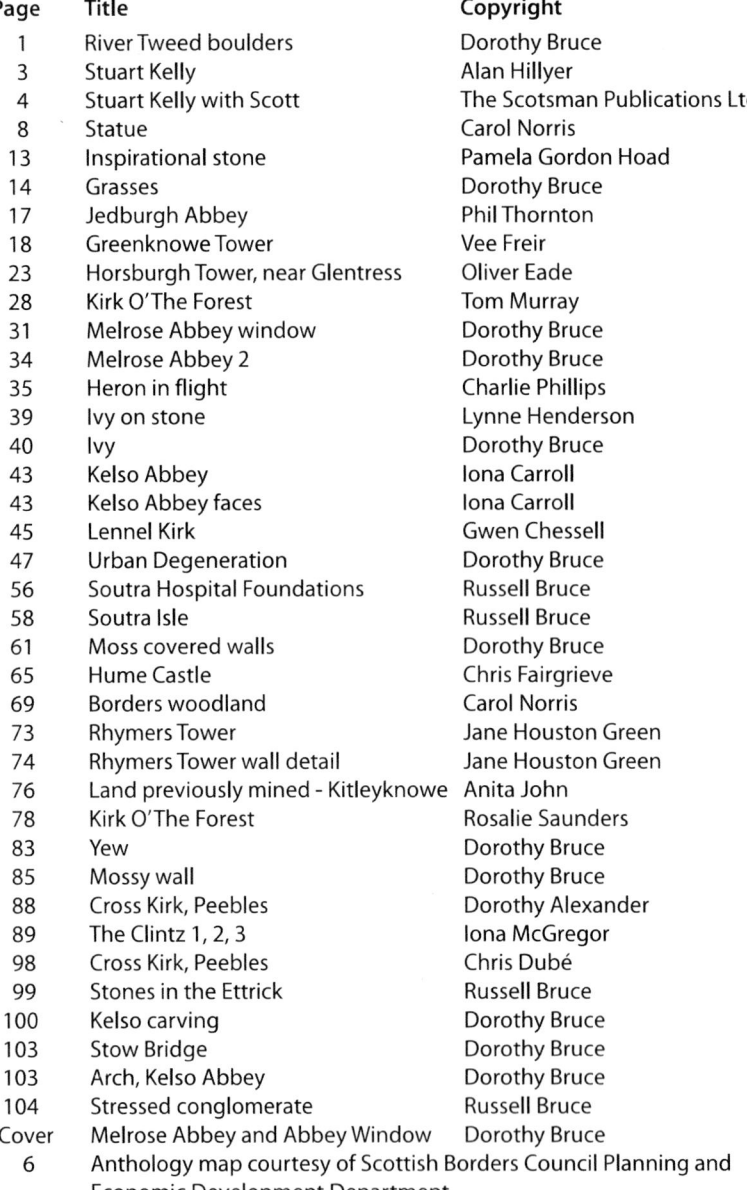

Stressed conglomerate

Credits

Page	Title	Copyright
1	River Tweed boulders	Dorothy Bruce
3	Stuart Kelly	Alan Hillyer
4	Stuart Kelly with Scott	The Scotsman Publications Ltd.
8	Statue	Carol Norris
13	Inspirational stone	Pamela Gordon Hoad
14	Grasses	Dorothy Bruce
17	Jedburgh Abbey	Phil Thornton
18	Greenknowe Tower	Vee Freir
23	Horsburgh Tower, near Glentress	Oliver Eade
28	Kirk O' The Forest	Tom Murray
31	Melrose Abbey window	Dorothy Bruce
34	Melrose Abbey 2	Dorothy Bruce
35	Heron in flight	Charlie Phillips
39	Ivy on stone	Lynne Henderson
40	Ivy	Dorothy Bruce
43	Kelso Abbey	Iona Carroll
43	Kelso Abbey faces	Iona Carroll
45	Lennel Kirk	Gwen Chessell
47	Urban Degeneration	Dorothy Bruce
56	Soutra Hospital Foundations	Russell Bruce
58	Soutra Isle	Russell Bruce
61	Moss covered walls	Dorothy Bruce
65	Hume Castle	Chris Fairgrieve
69	Borders woodland	Carol Norris
73	Rhymers Tower	Jane Houston Green
74	Rhymers Tower wall detail	Jane Houston Green
76	Land previously mined - Kitleyknowe	Anita John
78	Kirk O' The Forest	Rosalie Saunders
83	Yew	Dorothy Bruce
85	Mossy wall	Dorothy Bruce
88	Cross Kirk, Peebles	Dorothy Alexander
89	The Clintz 1, 2, 3	Iona McGregor
98	Cross Kirk, Peebles	Chris Dubé
99	Stones in the Ettrick	Russell Bruce
100	Kelso carving	Dorothy Bruce
103	Stow Bridge	Dorothy Bruce
103	Arch, Kelso Abbey	Dorothy Bruce
104	Stressed conglomerate	Russell Bruce
Cover	Melrose Abbey and Abbey Window	Dorothy Bruce
6	Anthology map courtesy of Scottish Borders Council Planning and Economic Development Department	